W9-AGM-500

Winners and Losers on the Russian Road to Capitalism

**Bertram Silverman and
Murray Yanowitch**

M.E. Sharpe
Armonk, New York
London, England

Library of Congress Cataloging-in-Publication Data

Silverman, Bertram.
New rich, new poor, new Russia: winners and losers on the Russian
road to capitalism / by Bertram Silverman and Murray Yanowitch.
p.   cm.
Includes bibliographical references and index.
ISBN 1-56324-704-6 (alk. paper). —
ISBN 1-56324-705-4 (pbk.: alk. paper)
1. Russia (Federation)—Economic conditions—1991—Congresses.
2. Wealth—Russia (Federation)—Congresses.   3. Poverty—Russia (Federation)—
Congresses.   4. Capitalism—Russia (Federation)—Congresses.
I. Yanowitch, Murray.   II. Title.
HC340.12.S55   1997
330.947'086—dc21   97-6665
CIP
Printed in the United States of America

The paper used in this publication meets the minimum requirements of
American National Standard for Information Sciences—
Permanence of Paper for Printed Library Materials,
ANSI Z 39.48-1984.

BM (c)   10   9   8   7   6   5   4   3   2   1
BM (p)   10   9   8   7   6   5   4   3   2   1

For Alice and Rose

Contents

List of Tables

Preface

This book had its origins in our efforts to bring together leading labor scholars, labor-management experts, and trade union leaders from the United States and Russia to examine the transformation of labor market institutions in our respective countries. Some of the contributions to these symposia were published in two earlier volumes that we jointly edited with Robert Vogt (*Labor and Democracy in the Transition to a Market System* [M.E. Sharpe, 1992]; and *Double Shift: Transforming Work in Postsocialist and Postindustrial Societies* [M.E. Sharpe, 1993]). Most of the U.S. contributors shared the view that economic performance in today's rapidly changing global economy depended on constructing more equitable and democratic ways of organizing human resources. One of the participants, former U.S. secretary of labor Ray Marshall, calls this newly evolving stage "human resource capitalism."

This study reveals that Russia has chosen a different road to capitalism. Guided by free market ideology, market reforms have resulted in dramatic declines in living standards that limit the forward movement of liberalization. As another participant in our symposia, labor economist Richard Freeman, warned, the ability to promote market reforms will ultimately depend on convincing the Russian people "to accept transitional costs while protecting them against the excesses of incipient capitalism."

But the success of market reforms in Russia also depends on how the costs and benefits of marketization are shared. In Russia, a deepening divide between winners and losers is becoming a major factor influencing the type of market system emerging in the post-Soviet period. This book examines the unequal distribution of the costs and benefits of reform, its impact on the changing social and economic structure of the population, and how these changes violate perceptions of equity and fairness.

While our focus is deliberately selective, our study does explore some of the principal concerns of the Russian people as they confront the realities of an emerging market system. In the chapters that follow we examine how the face of poverty has changed, and why many Russians, despite their earlier criticism of Soviet wage leveling, now have a negative view of widening wage differentials and sharply increasing social and economic inequality. We also look closely at the changing social and economic position of women and examine why they are among the principal losers in the reform process. Some Russians have of course benefited from market reforms. A new capitalist class has been created. We explore the principal social channels of recruitment of this class and what this suggests about changes in and continuities with Russia's Soviet past. Finally, our book concludes by addressing a puzzling question: Why has social democracy played such a limited role in reforming Soviet communism?

Readers will note that we have made extensive use of statistical materials issued by both official state agencies and nonofficial research organizations. Clearly, the far-reaching institutional changes and social turmoil associated with Russia's transition to capitalism were not always conducive to accuracy in statistical reporting. In the pages that follow, we alert readers to those instances in which questions have been raised about the reliability of the statistical reports and where marked discrepancies have appeared between official and nonofficial findings.

In the course of writing this book, we have turned to many Russian scholars for advice and assistance. Many of their names appear prominently in the pages that follow. We would especially like to express our gratitude to Leonid Gordon, Vladimir Gimpelson, Natalia Rimashevskaia, Tat'iana Zaslavskaia, Vladimir Iadov, Ovsei Shkaratan, and Vladimir Magun. Our numerous discussions with them and our access to their published and unpublished work have contributed significantly to our understanding of the major issues posed in this study. We are also especially indebted to Galina Manousova, who served as our research assistant in Moscow, and to Denis Sukhodolsky, our graduate assistant at Hofstra University. The dean of Hofstra University, Robert Vogt, a collaborator in our Russian projects, has continued to contribute to and support our work. Hofstra University has generously continued to support our research efforts. Patricia Kolb, executive editor at M.E. Sharpe, has played an invaluable role in encouraging and inspiring us to complete the book. Alice Kessler-Harris read the manuscript many times. Her critical voice pushed us to write more clearly and to avoid inconsistencies in presentation.

1

Free Market Ideology and the Specter of Inequality

As its surrounding satellites began to break free in 1989, the Soviet Union, to the surprise of most experts, seemed to implode. The defining conflict of the twentieth century, between communism and capitalism, ended, as T.S. Eliot might have said, "not with a bang but with a whimper." For the many who had lived under its oppressive yoke, the collapse of communism released a sense of new opportunities. Many of the restrictions on freedom were lifted, and suddenly it was possible to publicly voice grievances and preferences and to move more freely to pursue one's own interests. The strike movement and the emergence of political opposition groups suggested that a genuine civil society might find its place beyond the kitchen table to which previously it had been confined. To the extent that people were freer to follow their own interests, everyone has benefited from the fall of communism.

But lifting the constraints on liberty, what some have called negative freedom, was only one element in the experience of a newly emancipated population. In fact, there were losers as well as winners on the Russian road to capitalism. And in assessing their fate, positive freedom must command a great deal more attention.[1]

The positive aspects of freedom require social and economic conditions that make it possible for people to choose the life they wish to lead. Protecting civil rights is essential to allow individuals to be "free to choose." But without certain economic rights to protect their ability to choose, individuals are limited in their capacity to use their freedom. As Franklin Roosevelt warned in 1944, "necessitous men are not free men. People who are hungry and out of a job are the stuff of which dictatorships are made."[2]

Free market ideology pays little attention to the positive components of liberty. Yet, most actually existing market systems have in varying ways introduced a variety of social democratic rights that have promoted economic as well as political citizenship. They have usually done so in response to social and economic agitation. The history of capitalism is replete with the struggles of the "left-behinds" to gain greater economic and political rights to protect and use their freedom.

Three of the most important elements in achieving positive freedom are living standards, economic security, and equity. Poor people have little clout in either the marketplace or the political arena. And workers faced with limited financial resources and government support when unemployed, and with few prospects of finding new employment, have limited freedom to act in their own interests. How a society distributes income and wealth will also greatly influence the extent of positive freedom. If only a small minority has the economic resources to pursue its interests while the many have limited economic opportunity, the freedom of the majority will be significantly restricted. As Vaclav Havel has eloquently argued,

> the true aim of reform is to empower individual citizens. . . . [I]t comes very directly from better health. It comes from transferable job skills and a well functioning labour market which allow people some measure of power over their work. It comes from a measure of income security. Though some insecurity is inescapable in a market economy, extreme poverty and insecurity sap a person's identity and destroy his or her freedom.[3]

These elements of economic citizenship outlined by Vaclav Havel empower people to use both political and economic means to enhance the quality of life. Without a concept of economic rights, the positive aspects of freedom will be seriously undermined. The economist Albert Hirschman, in a pathbreaking book, has demonstrated how individuals use both "exit" and "voice" to improve the quality of their lives.[4] By exit, Hirschman means the use of one's "feet" (to expand his metaphor) to leave a job, a place, or product in search of something better. In contrast to exit, using one's voice is a political act. Rather than leaving a firm or a community, individuals choose to stay and express their discontents in order to improve their conditions. To be successful, voice frequently requires collective action to mobilize individual voices so they are more effectively heard.

But these channels of liberty depend on the flowering of positive freedom. Workers will not leave their jobs or raise their voices in protest if the cost of job loss is too great. The social protections provided by modern social democracies have not only enhanced the right to organize collectively but have reduced the potential costs of exit and voice and consequently have increased overall freedom. In the chapters that follow we seek to explore how the new market system in Russia has promoted or inhibited the development of positive freedom.

The Social Limits of Radical Reform

The ideology of free markets has guided the direction of Russia's turn to capitalism.[5] The radical reformers led by Egor Gaidar and his Western advisers engaged in a mission to demolish the bureaucratic command system by rapidly replacing it with the coercive powers of private property guided by the constraints of freely determined prices. They saw themselves as a "kamikaze cabinet" whose main purpose was to implement policies that would destroy the planning system and prevent the old communist nomenklatura from reestablishing their power.[6] The image of a kamikaze force engaged in a heroic attack mission that would result in its self-destruction tells us a great deal about the individuals and the ideology that guided Russia's second "revolution," a subject to which we return shortly.

The destruction has been great indeed. The hope and euphoria associated with the birth of negative freedom have faded. Rather than becoming an engaged and empowered citizenry, most Russians have withdrawn from politics and are increasingly skeptical that a weak state can protect them against the uncertainty of the marketplace and ensure the elementary safety of everyday life. For the majority of Russians the gift of freedom has been overwhelmed by the daily struggle to live. The long and ubiquitous lines that symbolized the wait for consumer goods have disappeared, replaced by high prices that keep the broad range of western products out of reach of the majority of ordinary citizens. In an ironic twist, Russians once again are asked to wait for the consumer bliss that a formerly despised capitalist economy is expected to bestow on them. Once again, radical reformers, now cloaked in free market ideology, place their faith in the heralded patience of the Russian people to postpone gratification and accept present sacrifices for a future that will turn Russia into a "normal" or "civilized" society.

The acceptance of short-run pain to achieve the benefits of future economic growth in both free market and communist ideology should not be surprising. Both belief systems place considerable emphasis on economic growth to achieve the good society. Free market ideology is particularly prone to promote the idea of market spontaneity to quickly push economic agents to respond to the requirements of economic growth. But in real life, adjustments to change take time and are costly. To reduce the pain of change, consideration needs to be given to the relationship between the rate of change and the time it will take to adjust to change. As Karl Polanyi noted in his classic study of the first transition to a market system, common sense should suggest that if the pace of change is too fast, it should be slowed down, if possible, to safeguard the welfare of the community.[7] He might also have added that the more privileged are always in a much better strategic position to accommodate to changing circumstances than less fortunate and vulnerable groups. Most Russians, regardless of their economic status, when asked about the pace of marketization, have repeatedly expressed the view that reforms should proceed more slowly.[8]

This symmetry of accepting short-run sacrifices for the sake of longer-term benefits reflects another commonality between free market liberalism and communist bolshevism: each is committed to destroying the past and as a consequence each underestimates the force of history in determining the future. The bolsheviks thought they needed to forcefully destroy the past in order to create a socialist future. But their inherited backward agricultural society played a decisive role in limiting economic development and in perpetuating a pseudo-socialist economy.

Efforts to reform the military-style command system have a long history. But unlike earlier attempts to reform the economy that failed to have a significant impact, Mikhail Gorbachev's perestroika and glasnost led to a severe economic crisis. By encouraging greater political and economic dissent and decentralization of economic decisions, Gorbachev hoped to create a real socialist society. One prominent reformer called it "the second socialist revolution."[9]

But perestroika weakened the centralized bureaucratic guidance system before workable market institutions were in place. And despite all the benefits of glasnost, greater freedom of expression and organization fatally undermined an already weakened and demoralized central authority. The center lost its effectiveness, not only because its functions were drastically curtailed, but because the authority of the Communist Party and the governing bureaucracy could be more easily defied. This set the stage for the beginning of an enormous growth in black and gray markets, theft, and official corruption.

The economic crisis that ensued pushed the leadership toward more radical economic solutions. Influenced by the collapse of communism in Eastern Europe and the growth of free market ideology in the West, Soviet economic thinking shifted increasingly away from pursuing some variant of democratic market socialism to the immediate construction of a market capitalist system to stem the tide of economic disintegration. When the Soviet Union collapsed in 1991, Boris Yeltsin turned to a youthful and relatively inexperienced group of economists and their Western advisers to resolve the economic crisis by quickly introducing capitalism.

The new radical economic reformers were not revolutionaries in the bolshevik mold. They could not destroy the past by force. Instead, their "shock therapy" was designed to replace the crumbling party and the state administrative command system by inventing a new future. Supporters of their policies were fond of quoting an old Chassidic injunction that "you can't cross a chasm in two leaps." By implication, building bridges between the old and the new was rejected, as was the possibility that a single leap might not get you to the other side. In their effort to jump into the future, everything in the past was rejected, and the past and the future were seen as ideological polar opposites: planning and state ownership were bad and needed to be destroyed, free markets and private property were good and needed to be quickly introduced.[10] Such an ideological stance is based on a fundamental fallacy. As the historian Robert Daniels observed,"it was as if the market could be invoked out of nothing as an instrument for the transition to the market itself."[11]

The metaphor of leaping a chasm suggests a number of other tenets of radical free market reform. On the other side, where free markets are supposed to reign, economies are guided by generally accepted economic principles that have universal applicability across nations. This leads to a strong belief in the power of economic knowledge to guide Russia down a proven and well-understood path to a market economy.[12] History and social institutions are largely ignored in radical reformers' economic analysis. In fact, history and society are seen as impediments that will be overcome naturally in the long run after sound economic policies are implemented.

In order to destroy the remnants of the administrative command system, Yeltsin quickly moved to radically transform the economy. Shock therapy rested on three main pillars: rapid liberalization of most prices and deregulation of enterprise activities to get prices right and to encourage increases in production in response to higher prices; restrictive fiscal and monetary policies to bring inflation under control and to impose stricter budgetary constraints on enterprises; and speedy privatization to break the links between firms and government and to encourage enterprise restructuring making it easier to enforce and sustain stabilization policies.[13]

The impact on most Russians was immediate and devastating. Inflation surged, real wages fell, and production declined beyond reformers' expectations. Overnight, Russians lost their savings and living standards plunged. More goods were visible in shops because higher prices drove ordinary Russians out of the marketplace. At the same time, domestic production collapsed because adequate distribution networks and coordinating mechanisms were not yet in place to replace the now defunct state planning systems. Production also fell because lower real wages reduced effective demand, which induced managers to reduce spending for capital goods and, not infrequently, to use their subsidies and credits to enrich themselves.

Stabilization policies were never systematically applied. Nor could they be. A weak government, parliamentary resistance, the fear of massive unemployment, and a "social explosion" politicized monetary and fiscal policies. The loss of government authority and effectiveness and the continued nexus between enterprises and the state helps explain why efforts to stabilize the economy were and remain so erratic. While the rate of inflation began to decline in 1995, for the vast majority budget balancing has meant deteriorating real wages, health care, and education, and increasing economic and social insecurity.

Privatization, the third pillar of reform, also produced unexpected results. The reformers succeeded in moving privatization forward very rapidly, but as we demonstrate more fully in Chapter 6, many of the chief winners were the old managers and nomenklatura. Many of the new private manufacturing and service enterprises have become engulfed in illegal and mafia-style activities. Despite efforts to democratize privatization through the distribution of vouchers and ownership shares to workers, a large proportion of the vouchers have ended up in the hands of speculators, and managers are becoming the effective owners of most former state enterprises. Nevertheless, recent studies suggest that managers of newly privatized firms are not acting like "theoretical capitalists" but still continue to follow older norms and goals.[14] It has become increasingly clear that Russia cannot recreate its economic and social institutions out of whole cloth. Rather, as the historian Moshe Lewin shrewdly suggests, the Russian economy and society can only be reinvented "from the given material, which consists of many past experiences, institutions, and traditions . . . ."[15]

Because the Gaidar team and its foreign economic advisers believed they could leap the chasm that separated Russia from other market systems, they became increasingly removed from the political process that surrounded them. Consequently, like the communists they sought to destroy, their top-down economic reforms increasingly isolated them from popular sentiments.[16] Those who criticized their policies were held to be ignorant of modern economic theory or not to have understood the policy alternatives they faced.[17] Unanticipated setbacks in the economy were attributed not to their policy failures—that is, to too much shock therapy—but rather to too little. They did not learn their lessons until the December 1993 election that routed them.

One lesson they might have learned is that market ideology provides little information about actually existing market systems. As Albert Hirschman has observed, "there is and always has been a large variety of 'really existing' market societies. This diversity helps to account for the shifting leadership of advanced industrial countries. . . . To opt for 'the market' thus does not mean to copy some uniform model of institutions and practices."[18] There is no simple way of determining why some market systems have performed better than others in different historical periods. The effectiveness of a market system is related to the institutional and organizational framework as well as the traditions and cultural values in which markets are embedded. Social norms and perceptions of fairness influence how economic actors and institutions respond to changes in the distribution of economic rewards.

Equality and Economic Performance

Once this premise is granted, one can no longer assume a priori what the relationship is between the performance of an economy and the degree of equality a market system promotes. The nexus between equality and economic performance is more complex than conventional economic theory or ideology suggests. Many economists now reject the traditional view that rising inequality is the price a society must pay for economic growth. Until recently, most economists accepted "Okun's Law," which asserts an inverse relationship or trade-off between efficiency and equity.[19] The Asian experience, however, suggests that today the converse may be closer to the truth.

There are a variety of reasons for believing that greater equality may promote growth and efficiency. In part, this shifting perspective reflects an increasing awareness of the role that investments in people play in economic growth.[20] More equal societies tend to invest a larger proportion of their income in the education and health of their populations. Less inequality also promotes greater incentives for the less fortunate to pursue education and to take risks. Finally, more equal societies tend to be more politically stable, enhancing the capacity of governments to engage in more effective economic policies. If the costs and benefits of government programs are more equally shared, larger numbers of people will be more willing to accept the sacrifices necessary to sustain economic growth. As the social policy analyst Isabel Sawhill has argued, the first principle of policymaking "is to compensate the losers."[21]

Radical reformers' rejection of a more egalitarian economic strategy may therefore be misplaced. The fear of equality reflected their apprehension that more populist social policies would ignite inflation. But their aversion to equality was also deeply rooted in their belief that communist egalitarianism played a major role in perpetuating the inefficiencies of the Soviet economy. This view was widely shared by the Soviet intelligentsia.

Yet Okun's Law does not seem to neatly fit the Soviet experience. The Soviet economy grew rapidly in the 1950s and through most of the 1960s. At that time economists such as Paul Samuelson were suggesting that Soviet-type planning systems might be a more effective way of promoting growth.[22] But this period of rapid growth was also associated with an accelerated decline in earnings inequality. Inequality began to increase quickly after 1968 and into the mid-1970s, at the very time that the Soviet economy began to stagnate.[23]

While the Soviet wage structure did not promote the efficient use of labor, the rise and fall of Soviet economic performance had less to do with trends in equality than with the institutional constraints of the planning system. Administrative command systems are more effective in mobilizing labor and capital than increasing their quality and productivity. Market systems typically have turned to centralized planning during wartime to mobilize and direct resources for military purposes. Soviet growth in the 1950s and 1960s was largely a consequence of increasing the quantity of labor and capital while continuing to restrict consumption. Circumstances changed in the 1970s. Increasingly, economic growth depended on improvements in the quality and productivity of capital and labor. Central planning was ill equipped to meet those challenges. Managers did not have the information, incentives, or capacity to improve productivity or the quality of their products.

Soviet wage differentials failed to adequately reflect work productivity and encourage the efficient use of labor. In this more limited sense, Soviet wage leveling and administrative wage determination contributed to poor worker performance. But reform of the wage structure to more accurately reflect workers' contribution to production should not be conflated with changes in the overall level of income and wealth inequality. Moreover, economists disagree about the factors determining wages in market systems. How wages are structured is one of the more contested subjects in modern economic theory. Many economists believe that wages and jobs are not like other prices and quantities but are influenced by "constraints arising from social norms."[24] Perceptions of fairness play an important role in influencing work performance and labor turnover. Increasing wage inequality in post-Soviet Russia has not contributed to a greater sense of fairness or to more effective work effort.

Russian reformers are fond of citing the early historical experiences of the United States and Britain to defend the increasing social and economic inequality in their country. They may be looking in the wrong places. Today, developing countries with the greatest inequality of wealth and income tend to be the poorest and least productive economies. On the other hand, some of the most successful, especially in East Asia, have relatively high levels of income equality and provide considerable economic security.

In a recent book on the transition process, Joseph Stiglitz, former chairman of President Clinton's Council of Economic Advisors, has argued that Russia and other East European economies have been more interested in efficiency considerations and have ignored their effect on income and wealth distribution. This neglect, he suggests, may come to haunt these economies not only in the form of social unrest but "more narrowly in terms of long-run economic inefficiencies.... [T]here is no intellectual foundation for the separation of efficiency and distributional concerns." And he concludes that "the former socialist economies are in the perhaps unique position of being able to obtain a degree of equality of ownership of wealth unattained and perhaps unattainable in other market economies.... [T]he challenge is to grasp the opportunity that it now provides to construct a more egalitarian society."25

The Specter of Inequality

Russia is moving along a different path—one haunted by the specter of inequality. As Russia painfully seeks to redefine its future, "a deep divide between winners and losers is emerging as the most important underlying factor in the country's struggle to move forward." That is the conclusion drawn from an extensive economic survey by the *Financial Times* in the spring of 1995.26 Many of the leaders of radical economic reforms are now expressing concern about the potential problems that these divisions are creating, and many intellectuals, who were in the early trenches in the battle against the deformities of Soviet communism, are now strongly critical of the strategy chosen to dismantle the Soviet system.

The deepening divide between winners and losers presents special problems when placed within the historical context of the Russian transition. First is the obvious fact that the overwhelming majority of Russians have lived in a society where the extremes of inequality did not exist or were hidden, and where open unemployment had been eliminated. Second, the rate of growth of inequality has been very rapid. In a period of four years Russia has ceased being a relatively equal society to become a society more unequal than any of its European or East Asian counterparts. While the level of inequality may still be greater in the United States, Russia has had little time to adjust to the rapid increase in the disparity of income and wealth (see Chapter 2). If the trend continues, the social and economic divisions in Russia will resemble those of a developing rather than a developed modern economy. Third, the economic success of a very small percentage of the population has occurred at a time when living standards of the average Russian have declined significantly and poverty has become a mass phenomenon (see Chapter 3).

Finally, there is one special feature of the growing social division that contributes greatly to the increasing uncertainty about the direction and meaning of the transition process: the paradoxical and often un-anticipated outcome of who is winning and who is losing in the transition to capitalism. For those who thought they would be winners and are now losers, the disappointments have been profound, especially when many of the new elites look like the old ones, and financial success often depends on criminal behavior and financial speculation rather than on the creation of real goods and services.

The differential impact of marketization on key social and economic groups is among our principal concerns in the chapters that follow. The divisions between the winners and losers are emerging as one of the most significant issues influencing the direction of market reforms. Which groups can be characterized as "winners," and which as "losers," in the economic transformation under way in the 1990s? What can we learn about the composition of the "new poor" and the "new rich" in Russian society? Is there persuasive objective evidence that supports the widespread view concerning the "erosion" or impoverishment of the "middle class"? To what extent have the "new rich" been drawn from the political elites of the Soviet era? What has happened to gender inequalities in economic status? Answers to these questions provide a way of revealing continuities with the Soviet past as well as changes taking place in post-Soviet Russia's unfolding market system.

2

Critical Responses to
Radical Reform

In seeking to destroy the communist system, radical reformers did not flinch from the social and economic dislocation that shock therapy inflicted on Russian society. Free market advocates believed that the disruptions offered a unique historical opportunity to speed the implementation of a fully formed market system. The sacrifices imposed on the Russian people were seen as a necessary cost of extirpating the nomenklatura as a ruling elite, and in so doing, making the reforms irreversible.

Radical reformers paid little attention to how the costs of reform would be shared or how to protect the losers. Their faith in the capacity of the market to raise living standards led them to underestimate the short-run costs of reform and to discount their long-term significance. As hardships continued into 1992 and 1993, they blamed them on the inherited deformities of the past and on the government's failure to fully implement the new economic policies. In the end, the reformers believed almost everyone would benefit as a more efficient and productive market economy raised Russia's standard of living.

It came as something of a shock, then, when the parliamentary elections of December 1993 resulted in a convincing defeat for the candidates grouped around the "Gaidar command." This was to be the first of a series of signals that a reappraisal of the reform strategy was in order. Early in 1994 several Russian publications—including both the journalistic and the more academic variety—carried some highly critical assessments of the consequences of the economic reform policies initiated at the beginning of 1992. These initial critical reactions formed the basis for a steadily escalating negative assessment of market reforms that were to follow.

Given the rather simplistic contrast between "reformers" and "hardliners" commonly invoked at that time in the Western press, it might be presumed that these critical assessments reflected the position of hardliners yearning for a return to the administrative-command system of the Soviet past. But such an assumption would be clearly mistaken. While there were obviously some differences among them, critics of the Gaidar reforms included some of the principal advocates for market-oriented reforms during the final days of the Gorbachev regime. Among them were economists like Stanislav Shatalin, Nikolai Petrakov, Leonid Abalkin, and Oleg Bogomolov, who had helped formulate Gorbachev's initial strategies for marketization.[1] Surveying the views of these critics illuminates the social and economic costs of reform and how those costs have been distributed.

Some of the critics made it clear that their evaluation of economic changes in 1992–93 was by no means wholly negative. After all, Shatalin and his colleagues noted, "the process of overcoming the total statization of the economy continued, and in many respects, accelerated." The critics applauded progress in creating an infrastructure for a market economy, acknowledging the appearance of "the first signs of competition." They recognized that a new generation of executives and entrepreneurs—"free of the burden of old dogmas and habits"—had begun to adapt to the functioning of the emerging market economy.[2] Yet, as they welcomed these changes, they remained deeply troubled by their costs.

They were, of course, right. Society had to pay a price for the reformers' market strategy, and in the view of most of the critics that price seemed clearly excessive. "The social cost paid by society for 'shock therapy' has exceeded the maximum permissible limits," wrote Shatalin.[3] Or, relying on somewhat different, but no less unambiguous rhetoric: "No goal, up to and including the promise of a new version of a 'radiant future,' can justify the social casualties that the chosen course has inflicted on Russian society."[4]

What were some of the costs (or "casualties") the critics had in mind? Among the more obvious were the substantial declines in aggregate output of goods and services, in the level of capital investment, and in the population's real income. But how extensive were these declines? Do they deserve to be characterized as "excessive"? Were they attributable directly to reformist policies initiated in 1992? How did they impact on the standard of living of the population? These are some of the questions this chapter addresses. As we proceed, it will become clear that the answers are not always clear cut. But the implementation of rapid economic liberalization was accompanied by a process critics labeled— perhaps with some justification—"mass impoverishment."

The Social Cost of Reform

Measurement problems make it difficult to get a precise estimate of trends in Russian economic performance. During the Soviet period output growth was frequently inflated, and after liberalization the sales and output of new private enterprises were hidden to avoid paying taxes. But recent efforts by the World Bank and the official Russian statistical agency (Goskomstat) to update the methodology by which gross domestic product (GDP) is calculated cast doubt on claims by some defenders of radical reform that aggregate output declines have been exaggerated.[5]

What do official estimates reveal about trends in aggregate output after the implementation of shock therapy? As Table 2.1 shows, GDP declined 22 percent between 1991 and 1993. By 1995 this measure of aggregate output had declined by 35 percent and fell an additional 5 percent in the first half of 1996—a cumulative annual drop of about 40 percent. Industrial production also declined precipitously, falling in 1995 to 54 percent of its 1991 level. By mid-1996 the cumulative annual decline in agricultural production had reached 40 percent. An even sharper decline in capital investment brought investment down in 1995 to 35 percent of its 1991 level, indicating that the country's future productive potential had been seriously damaged. The dramatic nature of the decline in aggregate output is captured when compared to the 31 percent fall of gross national product in the United States during the Great Depression.

But for "the man in the street" the most obvious cost of the marketizing reforms was a significant decline in living standards and the increased probability of falling into poverty. Claims of "mass impoverishment" that critics attributed to the Yeltsin–Gaidar reforms reflected the sharp increase in the proportion of the population whose income fell below the "minimum living standard" or "subsistence minimum" (*prozhitochnyi minimum*), the per capita income commonly

Table 2.1

Macroeconomic Indicators, Russia, 1991–1996

	1992	1993	1994	1995	1996 (first half)
Gross Domestic Product					
in % of 1991	85.5	78.1	68.2	65.5	
in % of preceding year	85.5	91.3	87.4	96.0	95.5
Industrial Production					
in % of 1991	82.0	70.7	55.4	54.4	
in % of preceding year	82.0	85.9	79.1	97.0	96.0
Agricultural Production					
in % of 1991	91.0	87.0	77.0	71.0	
in % of preceding year	91.0	96.0	88.0	92.0	93.5
Capital Investment					
in % of 1991	60.0	53.0	40.0	35.0	
in % of preceding year	60.0	88.0	76.0	87.0	86.0

Sources: Working Center for Economic Reform, Government of the Russian Federation, *Russian Economic Trends*, vol. 5 (1996), no. 2, pp. 78, 87; *Obshchestvo i ekonomika*, 1996, nos. 3–4, pp. 234–237.

recognized as the poverty threshold. Using official definitions of the poverty line, the data show that one-third or more of the population fell below this level in 1992–93, while the comparable figure for 1991 was some 11–12 percent. Although some nonofficial estimates suggest that these figures underestimate the true extent of impoverishment (an issue we review in the next chapter), there appears to be essential agreement among serious observers that any reasonable measure of the poverty threshold would show a significant increase in the proportion of the population below this line in the years following 1991.[6]

Critics who cited the pauperization of a significant proportion of the Russian population in 1992–93 as evidence of the excessive cost of marketizing reforms could—and did—also invoke related material pointing to a marked deterioration in the quality of life during this period: "A drastic marginalization of the population is taking place, and the numbers of poor, vagrants, alcoholics and drug addicts are growing. The quality of 'human material' is declining at a very fast pace (immunity against common disease is falling, and prostitution, venereal disease and births of children with congenital defects are on the rise)."[7] As we show shortly, there is certainly no scarcity of evidence suggesting a marked decline in the health of the population, including a sharp rise in infant mortality and a decline in life expectancy.[8]

Some supporters of radical reform dismiss the dismal image of social decline, maintaining that the standard of living has not fallen that much. The bleak picture painted by the critics was designed, they contend, to promote populist resistance to the radical reform of the economic system. Incomplete statistical information does make it difficult to provide a precise assessment of the social costs of the transition, but four years of reform is a long enough period to draw a general if somewhat partial picture of the impact of systemic reforms on living standards. Whether one wishes to label the declines in well-being as excessive or not, the evidence suggests that reformers underestimated the extent of the fall in the Russian standard of living.

Official statistics indicate that real wages had declined by 41 percent after the first year of shock therapy and had fallen an additional 14 percent by the end of 1995. After four years of reform, workers' average wages had declined by 55 percent. Falling real wages moved the average wage closer to the poverty line. In 1992 the average wage was three times greater than the poverty threshold; by 1995 it was only 1.8 times higher. Not only did average real wages decline rapidly, but enterprises increasingly delayed paying workers their wages on time. Clearly, full-time employment no longer protected many workers from falling into poverty.[9] These and other wage-related issues are more fully addressed in Chapter 5.

To make ends meet, some Russians have taken additional jobs to supplement their incomes. While the number of workers holding more than one job has increased since 1991, only 12–15 percent of the workforce in 1994 were so engaged.[10] But there are now also other means of earning income in the private or shadow economy that are not counted, and therefore the significance of multiple income sources may be higher than is reported. Consequently, the average income of wage and salary workers did not fall as sharply as average real wages.

The emergence of new forms of remuneration from property and entrepreneurship as well as pensions and transfer payments also need to be considered when estimating overall levels of compensation. Income from property and entrepreneurial activities was estimated to account for a larger percentage of total personal income than wages in 1995, representing 45 percent of total household income. Wages and

Table 2.2

Changing Patterns of Consumption

	1990	1991	1992	1993	1994	1995
Personal consumption (1991 = 100)		100	61	66	71	67
Household consumption as a percentage of GDP	47.4	43.4	34.3	40.2	39.7	—
Percent of consumption spent on food	36.1	38.4	47.1	46.3	46.8	—

Source: Goskomstat data published in Working Center for Economic Reform, Government of the Russian Federation, *Russian Economic Trends*, vol. 4, no. 1, p. 64, and vol. 4, no. 4, p. 56.

salaries made up only 39.5 percent of total income.[11] But the shifting composition of income tells us more about the changing distribution of income and wealth than it does about changes in the income of ordinary citizens. Few Russians have access to property or entrepreneurial ventures. For most Russians, wages still remain the major source of livelihood. But those Russians who do have access to private property are generating enormous incomes.

Pensions and other social benefits have also emulated declines in real average wages. In 1995 these social benefits represented 16 percent of total household income.[12] The average pension no longer provides adequate income to purchase basic necessities. For most of 1995 the value of the average pension fell below the official poverty line for pensioners.[13]

One would expect that personal consumption would not decline as sharply as real average wages. Households can draw on savings or borrow to sustain their standard of living. Nevertheless, as Table 2.2 reveals, personal consumption expenditure did fall by 39 percent in 1992 and in 1995 was still about one-third below its 1991 level. While consumption declined sharply in 1992, official statistics hide some real changes in the pattern of consumption that occurred before and after liberalization.

A visitor to Russia in 1991 and 1995 would have been struck by differences in the availability of consumer goods. In 1991, most retail outlets had few products to sell. A goods famine seemed to be evident everywhere. By 1995 conditions had changed dramatically. The ubiquitous queues that symbolized the rationing and shortages of the communist era had ended. Consumers could now choose from a surplus and variety of higher quality items frequently imported and no longer rationed or available only to more privileged groups.

But appearances also concealed other aspects of reality. In 1991, Russians fearful of impending shortages of consumer goods bought large quantities of goods and hoarded them in their homes. Thus, goods shifted from the store to the home rather rapidly. Conditions were different in 1995. Higher prices restricted the consumption of most ordinary Russians and so an apparent abundance of products was available in retail outlets. Goods were now more visible in the shops than in homes.

Nevertheless, official statistics do not take account of significant qualitative changes in consumption. Marketization had begun to correct the imbalance of power between consumers and producers that characterized the Soviet era. This was reflected in an increase in the quality of goods and services presented for sale. Nor do the official data take account of the barter and exchange in the private and "informal" sectors of the economy that are deliberately hidden from the tax collector. Bartering of services and household production of food and other goods for exchange has helped buffer some consumers from the impact of declining real wages and inflation. These changes in consumption and income have led many supporters of reform to suggest that declines in living standards have in fact been modest.

Yet as Russia approached the June 1996 presidential elections, some champions of reform began to acknowledge the seriousness of declining living standards and the threat they posed to political stability. Anatolii Chubais, the architect of privatization and a leading member of the Gaidar economic team, warned that the "real standard of living is so low that many Russians are desperate to believe in anyone who promises a better life."[14]

Public opinion surveys support the view of sharply falling living standards. Some of these perceptions are summarized in Table 2.3. When asked to evaluate changes in such quality of life indices as "life as a whole," confidence in the future, sense of freedom, personal security, family relations, material status of the family, and state of health, among others, Russians overwhelmingly expressed a negative view of their well-being. The majority of Russians believed that they

Table 2.3

Public Opinion Surveys: Public's Assessment of Various Aspects of Quality of Life

Aspects of quality of life	May 1991			October 1993		
	Responses in %			Responses in %		
	Positive assessment	Negative assessment	Coefficient of satisfaction[a]	Positive assessment	Negative assessment	Coefficient of satisfaction[a]
Life as a whole	57	33	0.70	48	44	0.63
Confidence in the future	26	64	0.61	21	69	0.49
Feeling of freedom	41	47	0.61	30	52	0.55
Personal security	46	47	0.63	25	68	0.50
Position in society	69	17	0.80	58	59	0.69
Level of education	60	38	0.75	56	36	0.70
Work as a whole	76	19	0.81	61	32	0.70
Relations in the family	83	9	0.88	73	19	0.77
Contacts with people	90	6	0.89	79	15	0.80
Free time	59	35	0.70	40	49	0.61
Material situation of family	33	60	0.56	25	73	0.48
Food supply of family	36	59	0.58	45	52	0.63
Housing conditions	59	40	0.72	53	44	0.62
State of health	59	37	0.71	51	46	0.63
Surrounding environment	37	61	0.58	38	54	0.56

Source: Larisa Zubova and Natalia Kovaleva, "The Quality of Life According to Subjective Estimates of the Population," *Ekonomicheskie i sotsial'nye peremeny: Monitoring obshchestvennogo mneniia,* 1994, no. 2, p. 42.

[a]The coefficient of satisfaction could vary from 0.25 ("completely dissatisfied") to 1.0 ("completely satisfied").

were better off before liberalization and they blamed the promoters of market reform for their economic distress.[15]

Popular perceptions of declining living standards partly reflect the inevitable uncertainties and frustrations Russians feel as they are asked to assimilate and adapt to new norms and values. But these subjective measures of well-being also reveal something more: a loss of the social and economic security that the Soviet state had provided. In focusing on the negative features of the Soviet era, radical reformers tend to depreciate Soviet communism's positive role in enhancing the well-being of ordinary Russians. As Amartya Sen noted in a recent essay, there is a tendency to "rubbish" what has been done before liberalization. "The potential force of a market economy rests," he notes, "on the social foundations of social changes that occurred under communism, including the gains in education, health care and the reduction of poverty."[16]

Under Soviet communism the Russian people endured the agony of political repression, limited economic opportunities and choice, poor pay, and pervasive bureaucratic inefficiencies and corruption. The human costs of the Soviet experiment were enormously high. Nevertheless, by the 1980s the state-regulated system ensured that virtually all of its citizens enjoyed a modest standard of living, job security, and price stability. Almost everyone had access to free education, health care, relatively early retirement, and diverse pensions and social benefits. Many state enterprises provided cheap housing, child care, vacation opportunities, inexpensive food, and other subsidies. A system of administrative prices made basic necessities such as food, children's clothing, housing, public transportation, and cultural activities affordable. Since the 1930s, most developed market economies also constructed welfare state systems to protect their citizens against market failures and the uncertainties of unregulated capitalism. This is not the path taken by Russian reformers.

Under the weight of market reform the foundations of the Soviet safety net have begun to break down. Reformers have been more attracted to the free market attributes of capitalism than to the social democratic features of most already existing market systems. Many reformers viewed the Soviet safety net as undermining efficiency and modernization, a relic of the past that needed to be radically modified. In paying more attention to liberalization and less to social protection and to the rebuilding of social welfare institutions, the major pillars of the Soviet social security system began to crumble and most Russians lost the guarantees that had protected their standard of living.

Inflation has sharply increased the cost of basic necessities. As real wages declined, Russians were forced to curb consumption and alter what they consumed. As Table 2.2 reveals, the proportion of household consumption expenditures as a percentage of GDP declined in 1994 to 39.7 percent from its 1990 level of 47.4 percent. During the Soviet era the relatively low proportion of consumption expenditures in GDP came to symbolize the restricted power of the consumer under communism. By this measure their power had eroded even further. While the proportion of GDP devoted to consumption rose in 1993, in 1994 it was still almost 4 percent below its immediate pre-reform level.[17]

Inflation also destroyed household savings, preventing most Russians from drawing on past income to sustain current consumption levels. As a consequence, many families were forced to sell whatever assets they possessed in order to get by. Additional income from second jobs and food produced on private plots helped, but were not the main source of sustenance that kept many from slipping into poverty. Family networks and help from neighbors and friends have been a more significant source of assistance. Without family income transfers and other informal support networks, the impact of declining real income would have been much worse. According to a Russian Longitudinal Monitoring Survey undertaken by the World Bank in collaboration with Goskomstat, private transfers averaged 40 percent of recipients' household income and brought their poverty rates down by 10 percent in comparison with those who did not have access to such assistance.*[18]

Despite these informal support systems, the majority of Russians have been forced to spend more of their income on food, leaving relatively little for nonfood consumption. The quality of food consumption has deteriorated as well. As Table 2.4 reveals, by 1994 Russians were consuming less milk, vegetables, meat, and fish and eating more bread and potatoes. This is another clear index of the increasing impoverishment of the Russian people.

But stringent government budget constraints have limited the government's ability to respond to social distress. At a time of rapidly falling living standards, overall spending on social protection as a pro-

---

*Marketization has also changed the pattern of intrafamily support. Under Soviet communism, younger families received assistance from their usually better-off parents. Today it is more common for elderly pensioners to be supported by their children, especially the more fortunate who engage in successful new businesses.

Table 2.4

Consumption of Selected Food Items (physical quantities, per capita)

	1990	1991	1992	1993	1994
Meat and meat products (kg)	69	63	55	54	53
Milk and milk products (kg)	386	347	281	294	278
Eggs (units)	297	288	263	250	234
Fish and fish products (kg)	20.3	15.8	12.3	11.9	10.0
Sugar and confectionary (kg)	47.2	37.8	30.0	31.0	31.0
Vegetables (kg)	89	86	77	71	65
Fruit (kg)	35	35	32	29	n.a.
Bread and bread products (kg)	119	120	125	124	124
Potatoes (kg)	106	112	118	127	122

Source: Centre for Co-operation with Economies in Transition, *OECD Economic Surveys: The Russian Federation* (Paris, 1995), p. 124.

portion of GDP declined by 5 percent between 1992 and 1994.[19] Despite the spread of poverty, the real value of cash benefits and consumer subsidies has fallen sharply. As the Organization for Economic Cooperation and Development (OECD) notes, "there appears to be no relationship between social needs and the level of social benefits."[20]

The social safety net has eroded too quickly to effectively respond to declining living standards. The official minimum wage has been adjusted irregularly. After accounting for inflation in 1995, it was equal to 20 percent of its 1991 level and to only 7 percent of the average wage. For most workers, the minimum wage is no longer an instrument for protecting their income. The wages of workers in the "budget sector" (those who are paid directly by the government, including employees in central and local government administration, education, health care, research, and cultural services) are determined by changes in the minimum wage. As a result of the falling value of the minimum wage, the real wages of these workers, many of whom are highly skilled professionals, have deteriorated relative to other less-skilled workers. Moreover, some cash benefits such as family allowances, minimum unemployment benefits, pensions paid to those who have never worked, and disability pensions are also scaled to the minimum wage. As a result, the welfare of families that depend on such benefits has also declined.

The end of the Soviet commitment to full employment adds a new dimension to economic insecurity that also contributes to declining living standards. By mid-1996 unemployment reached 9.1 percent of the labor force.[21] Delayed wage payments, forced leaves, and reduced hours of work are hidden forms of unemployment that obscure its real level. These issues are considered in greater detail in Chapter 5. While the more open form of unemployment has not yet reached the dire levels predicted by some critics, it does pose special problems for many Russians. Families without a breadwinner tend to be excluded from many family support programs. Many of those cash benefits are distributed at the workplace, and bureaucratic difficulties make it difficult to collect them at the place of residency. Moreover, the real value of unemployment benefits are so low that most of the unemployed do not bother to register with the employment service to receive them.

The rapidly eroding safety net is clearly evident in the deterioration of the health care system. Responsibility for health care (and a variety of social assistance programs) has been transferred from the central to the provincial and local governments. But the shift did not bring with it a comparable transfer of funds. The inevitable fiscal squeeze has reduced the quality of health care and other social services. Since 1993, free health care is available only to old-age pensioners, war invalids, and children under three. Higher quality medical services are beyond the means of most families. The fiscally starved public sector provides only the most basic services. Low-paid professionals working with limited medical supplies and poor equipment have contributed to the declining health of the Russian people.

Sharply declining longevity provides compelling evidence of the deterioration of the population's health. Within a period of less than four years the life expectancy of men declined from 63.5 to 57.3 years. Less dramatically, women's life expectancy fell by three years during the same period. Infant mortality rates have also increased, and the annual death rate between 1990 and 1994 increased by 40 percent (see Table 2.5).

Curiously, some supporters of free market reform reject the prevailing view that declining living standards constitute a principal cause of increasing mortality and morbidity. Instead they claim that Russia's increasing death rate is related primarily to the growing stress of everyday life.[22] But stress is also a response to sharply falling living standards and to a pessimistic outlook about future prospects. Such negative feelings are clearly reflected in public opinion polls and are reinforced by the increase in suicides and alcoholism. It seems more

Table 2.5

Indicators of Health, Russian Federation

	1990	1991	1992	1993	1994
Life expectancy at birth					
Men (years)	63.8	63.5	62.0	58.9	57.3[a]
Women (years)	74.3	74.3	73.8	71.9	71.1[a]
Mortality (per 1,000 inhabitants)	11.2	11.4	12.2	14.5	15.7
Infant mortality (per 1,000 live births)	17.4	17.8	18.0	19.9	18.6
Nutrition (daily per capita calorie intake)	2,589	2,527	2,438	2,552	2,427[a]

Source: Goskomstat data published in Centre for Co-operation with Economies in Transition, *OECD Economic Surveys: The Russian Federation* (Paris, 1995), p. 123.
[a]Preliminary.

reasonable to view the evidence of sharply increasing death rates as an additional indicator of a society undergoing dramatic declines in living standards.*

Distributing the Cost of Reform

Despite the many differences between critics and supporters of radical reform, there is one issue on which both seem to agree. They share a negative assessment of the increasing inequality in the distribution of income that has accompanied the reform process. These trends suggest that however one measures the aggregate cost of reforms, the burden of these costs has been distributed in a highly unequal manner among the principal social groups in Russian society.

Official measures of income distribution indicate how quickly Russia has been transformed from a relatively equal society to one with considerable income disparities. The Gini coefficient, a general mea-

---

*Vladimir Magun, a Russian social psychologist, claims that his research team found that feelings of stress are more prevalent among women than among men, although life expectancy is significantly lower among men.

sure of inequality, rose from 0.26 in 1991 to 0.38 in 1995, an increase of 46 percent.* The Russian Center for Public Opinion Research reported a Gini coefficient of 0.46 in 1994. The gap between the average income of the highest 10 percent and the lowest 10 percent of the income recipients increased even more sharply, rising from 3.44 times in 1991 to 14.3 in 1994, and decreasing slightly to 13.5 in 1995.[23]

The rapid growth of inequality has provided little time for Russians to adjust to these dramatic changes in social and economic differentiation. Comparisons with other countries demonstrate the extent of these changes. Inequality in Russia is now much higher than in Western Europe and falls within a range of countries, such as the Philippines, with highly unequal distributions of income. The growing disparity of income during a period of declining living standards exacerbates feelings of increasing deprivation.

Clearly such increases in inequality were not what most critics of communism had in mind when they advocated changing the Soviet distributional system. During the final years of Soviet rule, most reformers, even many advocating some form of market socialism, accepted the need to increase inequality based on differences in skills and work performance. Thus, for example, Tat'iana Zaslavskaia stressed that "the trend towards growing income differentials is a natural phenomenon and one that is useful to society."[24] Gennadii Lisichkin—another prominent supporter of market-oriented reforms during this period—argued that the assessment of work performance, and hence the fixing of wage differentials, should be entrusted "not to the State Committee on Labor but to the market."[25]

Zaslavskaia and Lisichkin reflect the negative assessment by Soviet-era reformers of the "wage-leveling" and "egalitarianism" that had long affected Soviet wage-fixing practices and attitudes. A particularly strong critic of Soviet "egalitarianism," Natal'ia Rimashevskaia, regarded "the many years of implementation of the doctrine of egalitarianism" as the principal cause of the deterioration of the quality of the workforce in the final years of Soviet rule (as evidenced by "processes of deprofessionalization, the loss of work skills and the capacity for intensive and systematic work and . . . initiative").[26] While there were occasional appeals in the late 1980s for the redistribution of income

---

*The Gini coefficient can range from 0 to 1. The higher the coefficient, the greater the level of inequality.

from the top downward, they were clearly exceptional. The principal message conveyed in the literature on this subject was the dysfunctional nature of "egalitarianism" and the positive consequences of increased wage and income differentials.

But when the increased inequality in the distribution of income that accompanied the Gaidar–Yeltsin reforms of 1992–93 became apparent, it was certainly not welcomed—either by the critics of these reforms cited earlier (Shatalin, Abalkin, etc.) or by the reforms' principal defender (Egor Gaidar himself). Why should the consequences of the long-hoped-for abandonment of "egalitarianism" and "wage-leveling" have elicited such widespread negative assessments—at least in the published economic literature?

In some respects, the answer seems perfectly obvious. Neither the critics of "wage-leveling," nor for that matter anyone else with a modicum of concern for social justice, could be expected to celebrate a situation in which the chief casualties of an economic environment characterized by substantial declines in national output and real income included the lowest income groups in Russian society. But that was precisely the situation implied by the sharp increases in inequality in the distribution of income in 1991–95. To make the same point somewhat differently: it is hardly surprising that there should be widespread criticism of policies generating a pattern of income distribution in which upper-income groups were deriving an increasing share of a sharply declining "social pie." Thus, when critics of the Gaidar–Yeltsin reforms of 1992–93 (like Shatalin and Abalkin) cited evidence of increased income inequality as illustrative of the negative consequences of these reforms, it seemed unnecessary to spell out in any detail the grounds for such a negative assessment. It seemed perfectly obvious that an approximately 40 to 50 percent decline in the real income of the population, accompanied by sharply increased income differentials, had "aggravated the social situation in the country."[27]

But some of the critical literature in this area focused on specific features of the emerging pattern of income distribution that appeared particularly troubling. Quite apart from the negative connotations of an increasing gap between relatively high and low income groups in the midst of sharp economic decline, a considerable range of observers was especially disturbed by what appeared to be the sad fate of the former Russian middle class. As Rimashevskaia put it in an interview conducted early in 1994:

> It is especially alarming that the "center" is dissolving. It seems to me that while some are going into business and becoming rich, a large proportion is becoming impoverished. The middle class is eroding. . . . As we know, the middle class is the bulwark of any state. This is that stable group that is engaged in production, that makes it possible to master new technology, to treat and to teach people, to ensure future development.[28]

A similar concern with the fate of the middle class was sounded by Iurii Sukhotin of the Central Mathematical Economics Institute. Sukhotin argued that the increase in the proportion of the population below the official poverty line was fueled primarily not by "marginals" but by a considerable number of people drawn from "the most valuable cadres, the bulwark and hope of modernization"—students; personnel employed in medicine, science, and education; skilled workers; and technicians at enterprises that had failed to adapt to the "difficult economic regime of the transition period."[29]

This concern with the polarization of income and the allegedly disproportionate costs imposed by the market transition on groups loosely characterized as the "middle class" was not confined to critics of the reform process. Indeed, the principal architect of the Russian government's reform program, Egor Gaidar, appeared to share the negative assessment of these trends in income distribution.

In an article published at the end of 1993, Gaidar distinguished between the costs associated with declining output and those associated with growing inequality. According to Gaidar, declines in output did not impose particularly significant costs on the Russian people. After all, much of the decline in production reflected reductions in the output of armaments and in the branches that served this sector, as well as in types of goods that could not be justified in a market economy.* Moreover, the experience of other crisis-ridden economies undergoing similar transformations suggested to Gaidar that declines in output of 30–40 percent were normal in such situations.

Gaidar then turned to what appeared to him as a more troublesome feature of the reform process. "In my view, an immeasurably more

---

*Of course, workers and professionals, many highly skilled, and employed in this sector experienced significant declines in their living standards. Without a strategy to reemploy them, declines in the military–industrial branches of the economy do impose significant social costs on the population.

serious cost of the transformations begun under such difficult circumstances has been the sharp growth in the differentiation of incomes."
But he was quick to note that this, like the decline in output, also
seemed unavoidable. "The launching of market mechanisms always
leads to the short-term growth of differentiation."[30] Yet what did seem
particularly disturbing to the leader of radical reform was the sharp
decline in the real incomes of "large, traditionally middle-income population groups."

Having acknowledged all this, Gaidar was quick to warn that "additional lavish social programs" would not help solve the problems associated with declining real incomes and their increasingly unequal
distribution. The solution could only be found in restoring economic
growth. To do this required creating an environment favorable to private investment, and this necessitated, above all, "monetary stability,
low inflation, low interest rates, moderate taxes, and a reliable legal
base that would guarantee private property." All these policies had to
be joined to a general approach that sought to divest the state of "functions that were inappropriate for it under conditions of a market."[31]

Few of the critics of radical reform, whose work we briefly reviewed, called for anything that might appropriately be characterized
as "lavish social programs." They did appeal, however, for a general
approach that would "combine economic effectiveness and social justice," that would provide "selective support for priority spheres" of the
economy, and that would establish certain "social guarantees" (for
example, a guaranteed "subsistence minimum," and a minimum share
of expenditures on education and health care in GNP) that could not be
violated under any condition.[32]

Most critics, however, have not linked the problems of growing
inequality to issues of efficiency. The sociologist Nina Naumova is one
of the few who has attempted to do just this. In her view, augmenting
equality of opportunity not only encourages greater efficiency but is
also necessary for preserving democratic institutions. Developing a
viable middle class is central to Naumova's analysis.

The importance of strengthening the middle-class base was not a
new theme in Russian discussions of this period, but Naumova's formulation was unusually direct and wide ranging: "Only a strong and
numerous middle class can serve as a bulwark of reform, ensuring not
only political support, but above all—economic growth and the economic effectiveness of reforms." The formation of such a class rested

not on individual mobility but on the vertical mobility of whole strata, which in turn required real "equality of opportunity." Naumova repeatedly emphasized the latter point. "Hence the task of social policy in a modernizing society is to equalize opportunities, to expand the range of people having genuinely equal socioeconomic chances." But equality of opportunity depended on social policies that reduced poverty and expanded equal access to such social goods as education, culture, and health care. Unless such policies are implemented, the economic performance of the majority of the population will not be stimulated.

Naumova's repeated invocation of this principle of equal opportunity (which, she noted, was "not even being posed" by current authorities) pointed out that exactly the opposite was now occurring in Russian society. For example, the growth of paid education certainly heightened the differentiation of opportunities for young people. Moreover, what Naumova regards as the "programmed" mass impoverishment embedded in current economic reforms threatened to create a highly polarized society in which wealth and income differentiation would be carried to "an extreme."[33]

Lack of confidence in the new economic elite exacerbated critics' apprehensions about the spread of poverty. Negative images of Russia's emerging capitalist class reinforced popular mistrust of the new rich and contributed to perceptions that the costs of change were being unfairly distributed. Iurii Sukhotin, among the most scathing of critics, observed with dismay that while an increasing proportion of the population now lives below the poverty line,

> it is no secret that at the opposite pole of the income pyramid there are the anti-social elements (parasitical compradors and "parasites on parasites"—racketeers and other criminal bigwigs) employed not in the creation but in the wasteful appropriation . . . of created wealth, of produced goods, thereby stifling the useful efforts of creative strata of entrepreneurs and commodity producers.[34]

Only individuals in the top decile of the income distribution in the early post-Soviet period, according to Sukhotin, experienced an increase in real purchasing power. Given the significant role in the top decile of the "anti-social elements" cited in the above quotation, the unjust nature of current trends in income distribution must have seemed all the more obvious to Sukhotin. Other critics, such as Natalia

Rimashevskaia, were disturbed that the new rich now had at their disposal creature comforts that were not available even to the highest levels of the party nomenklatura in the days of Soviet rule.[35]

It would be a mistake to regard these views as simply reflecting the egalitarian heritage of decades of Soviet rule. For example, it is worth recalling Rimashevskaia's unambiguous critique of Soviet-era egalitarianism (see p. 27). For Rimashevskaia as well as for Naumova and Sukhotin and many other critics, it was not simply the increased income inequality but the dysfunctional (or even irrational) nature of the evolving income structure that was disturbing. Why should the development of a market economy be accompanied by the impoverishment of the "middle class" and the enrichment of social groups that could hardly be regarded as contributing significantly to the production of goods and services? Could it be that in some respects the transition to a market economy might actually limit the access of capable individuals in lower-income groups to "middle-class" positions? Might not the continuation of current trends in income distribution reduce political support for the continuation of marketizing reforms?

These were some of the questions implicit in the critical literature briefly reviewed above . Such issues were no less a part of the intellectual discourse on the distribution of the costs (and benefits) of economic reforms than the following unavoidable questions: Was it not obviously unjust that the real income of the least well off part of the population was declining much more rapidly than that of the population as a whole?[36] And as the sociologist Z.T. Golenkova asked: "How can such disparities be justified if they bear little relationship to labor productivity and output"?[37]

Large sections of the Russian population agreed. Public opinion surveys on this matter in 1993–94 reveal that Russians shared the experts' critical perceptions of emerging patterns of income inequality. More than three-quarters of respondents in these surveys regarded the current distribution of income as unjust, a view that predominated "among all groups of the population, regardless of socio-occupational status, type of main employment, sector of economy, place of residence, and level of income."[38]

Clearly, the prevalence of these sentiments does not simply reflect the continuing impact of Soviet-era egalitarian ideology. Indeed, the surveys show that only about a quarter of respondents favored the principle of an equal distribution of income. A distinct majority ap-

Table 2.6

Public Opinion Survey: Which Groups Have the Greatest Opportunity to Increase Their Income? (% of respondents)

	Year of survey		
Responses	1990	1992	1993
Members of cooperatives	68	55	42
Swindlers and manipulators	65	62	66
Personnel in trade and service sector	41	35	27
Personnel in state apparatus (nomenklatura)	24	14	20
New businessmen, dealers in securities	—	32	41
People with initiative, entreprising people	19	20	18
Leaseholders, private farmers	18	14	7
Directors of state enterprises	19	16	41
Specialists, engineering-technical personnel	3	2	3
Workers	1	1	1
Collective farmers, state farm personnel	2	2	0

Source: L.A. Khakhulina, "The Attitude of the Population to the Differentiation of Incomes and Social Stratification," *Ekonomicheskie i sotsial'nye peremeny: Monitoring obshchestvennogo mneniia*, 1993, no. 4, p. 8.

The size of the sample was 1,380 in 1990, 1,079 in 1992, and 1,880 in 1993.

peared to believe that an egalitarian income distribution was compatible with "incentives for effective work."[39] What did seem unfair to many Russians was not the inequality of income as such, or even the recent increase in income inequality, but who was losing and who was winning in the transition to capitalism.

Most of those surveyed believed that the principal beneficiaries of the early stages of the market transition were groups characterized as "swindlers and manipulators"—a characterization roughly similar to that used by Sukhotin to describe individuals in the upper decile of the income distribution (see Table 2.6). Fully two-thirds of respondents in a 1993 public opinion survey agreed with this characterization of the principal winners in the course of economic reforms. No more than 1 to 3 percent of respondents regarded workers, collective and state farmers, and engineering-technical personnel as the main beneficiaries. Among the groups ranking close to "swindlers and manipulators" were directors of state enterprises, new entrepreneurs, and securities dealers (*birzheviki*). Other surveys conducted in the same year showed that "diligent work and talent" were regarded as less likely to contribute to riches than "dishonesty" and "connections with the necessary people," and that only one out of five respondents agreed that "ordinary people" had been given opportunities to increase their incomes recently.[40]

To some degree these sentiments and perceptions undoubtedly bear the stamp of old ideological stereotypes and traditional Soviet suspicions of the origins of "big money," and of the practices frequently necessary to achieve career success in the old days. But surely these perceptions also reflect the differential impact of the early stages of the market transition on the lives of the principal social, occupational, and demographic groups in Russian society.

Supporters of radical reform view the causes and solutions to problems of income inequality quite differently. They acknowledge the troublesome trend of shifting the burden of reform onto the shoulders of the poorest social groups. But in their view this disturbing problem is not the result of radical economic reforms; rather, it is a consequence of rapid inflation. Had more rigorous financial controls been enforced, a policy they advocated, the poor would have suffered less. As the economists Brigitte Granville, Judith Shapiro, and Oksanna Dynnikova argue, statistical evidence reveals a very high correlation between poverty and inflation growth. Rapid inflation increases poverty because, unlike the rich, the poor have a limited ability to shift income and assets to protect themselves from rapidly rising prices. "Higher inflation," they contend, "hurt the very people whom populist demagogues and the simply confused seek to help."[41] The best way to help the poor and reduce the disparities in income is to lower the rate of inflation growth by imposing stricter financial controls. According to Granville, Prime Minister Viktor Chernomyrdin's renewed commitment in 1995 to financial stabilization has already brought results. Inflation has moderated and, as a result, poverty and income inequality have begun to fall. A vicious cycle of high inflation and increased poverty has been replaced with a "virtuous" one.[42]

Few critics of reform would deny that inflation has inflicted an unfair burden on the poor. Nor would many disagree with the view that effective macroeconomic stabilization is a necessary element in containing inflation. But inflation is not the only cause of declining real income. The sharp fall in aggregate output and productivity has also played a significant role in reducing living standards. Financial stabilization policies have contributed to the depression in output. Monetary policies have kept interest rates at very high levels. While they have declined in tandem with the reduction in inflation, in early 1996 real interest rates on short-term government bonds were still in the neighborhood of between 40 and 50 percent. High interest rates encourage the flow of funds into financial assets rather than into plant and equipment and other forms of productive capital. The sharp decline in capital investment is one of the major factors perpetuating declining productivity and living standards.

Another issue not discussed in Granville, Shapiro, and Dynnikova's analysis deserves special attention: how government taxing and spending influence who wins and who loses in efforts to control inflation. Budgets involve both taxing and spending. The new private sector and the rich have evaded paying taxes. Political influence and corruption have also reduced revenues. As a result, greater emphasis has been placed on spending cuts. The burden of reduced government spending has fallen heavily on the weak. As the economist Grigory Yavlinsky noted early in the reform process, the government gives "to everyone who is strong. . . . [T]hey weren't afraid of teachers, doctors, culture and science . . . so they didn't give them anything."[43]

Spending cuts on health care, education, and social protection have contributed significantly to the decline in the Russian standard of living. Public investments in health, education, and living standards are important elements in evaluating macroeconomic policies. The economist Amartya Sen touches on some of these issues in a recent essay on economic policy and offers a different perspective on market reform than those developed by Granville and other defenders of radical reform. Investments in what economists call "human capital," Sen argues, have

> practical importance . . . in promoting economic growth and through it further advancing the quality of life people can enjoy. While the improvement of human life is its own reward, it also offers—as it happens—other rewards which in turn can create the possibilities of further augmentations of the quality of life and our effective freedom to lead the lives we have reason to seek.[44]

In Sen's "virtuous circle," in sharp contrast to the version offered by Granville, reformers are asked to consider a wider range of issues when formulating financial stabilization policies, and it is suggested that government has a positive role to play. To extend social opportunities, he argues, "requires much more than the 'freeing' of markets."

It calls for an active role for government aimed at expanding positive freedom, that is, the capacity to participate in the new opportunities that a market system offers.[45]

The political resurgence of the Communist Party in the December 1995 elections pushed the issues of declining living standards and growing inequities to the forefront of political and economic debates. In his State of the Nation address on February 16, 1996, Boris Yeltsin belatedly recognized the importance of confronting the concerns of losing groups. He admitted that "the government, which is focusing on financial stabilization, has forgotten about people living on wages and pensions." And he warned that "the government will either carry out its duty to defend the social and economic rights of people or this will be done by another government."[46] The spectacle of Boris Yeltsin promising to pay back wages and to increase retirement pensions in exchange for votes suggested that political expediency, rather than coherent social programs, was guiding social policy. Nevertheless, losing groups were beginning to influence policy. As the journalist Thomas Friedman observed, "the left-behinds" were "starting to challenge the winners."[47]

In the next chapter we turn our attention to the most vulnerable, the poor. In the Soviet period the poor were mainly drawn from the weaker segments of society: the young, the old, the ill. Marketization has changed this. A new form of poverty has emerged. The sociologist Leonid Gordon calls it the poverty of the strong.

3

The Rise of Mass Poverty

There is no freedom without financial means.
—Aleksandr V. Zolin

In a volume published in 1979, Alastair McAuley, a leading British scholar of Soviet living standards and income distribution, noted that "Soviet authors do not use the Russian word for poverty to describe the conditions of the least well-off families in the USSR."[1] This Soviet-style inhibition would remain in effect for another nine or ten years, until the spirit of glasnost had thoroughly permeated the country's economic discourse.

However, it would be a mistake to assume that the subject of domestic poverty began to be discussed by Soviet social scientists only in the late 1980s. The Soviets used a variety of alternative terms that suggested some of the changing ideas about poverty. The concept of a "subsistence minimum"—essentially a poverty threshold—and the kinds of family budgets that were required to meet this minimum could be found in the Soviet economic literature early in the postrevolutionary period. Introduced into Soviet economic discussions shortly after the Bolshevik revolution, minimum subsistence wages and subsistence budgets were developed primarily for industrial workers. But as a result of a deepening economic crisis the subsistence minimum was redefined to include only a selection of food items.[2] After the collapse of communism, the new Russian government would also change the criteria for measuring poverty.

The concept of a subsistence minimum essentially disappeared from the literature in the 1930s and through the early postwar years (after all, with socialism—or at least its "foundations"—allegedly in place, it hardly seemed appropriate to calculate a poverty threshold). However, the concept was revived in the period of the Khrushchev "thaw" of the late 1950s and early 1960s. During this period, in addition to a "current" minimum, economists developed two additional budgets that projected much higher subsistence thresholds.[3] Explicit references to domestic "poverty" *(bednost')*, nevertheless, remained taboo until the late 1980s. But most readers (both Western and Soviet) surely understood that when Soviet writers referred to families with "scanty resources" or families that were "not sufficiently provided for" *(maloobespechennye)*, they had in mind, quite simply, groups that under Soviet circumstances could legitimately be classified as poor.

Among the principal functions served by Soviet studies of subsistence minimums was the derivation of a data base that would permit the establishment of minimum wage rates, minimum pensions, and family income supplements. Drawing on such material, McAuley estimated that in 1967–68 about 35–40 percent of the Soviet population had per capita incomes that (in the coded language of those days) could be considered below the official poverty level.[4] Commonly cited estimates of the poverty threshold in the mid-1970s and the 1980s suggest that the officially designated poor constituted some 15–20 percent of the Soviet population in this period.

Table 3.1 shows the figures that have appeared in the Russian literature as the poverty threshold for several years between 1975 and 1989, along with our estimates of the proportion of the population with incomes below these threshold figures. For 1975 and 1985 the poverty line is taken as the equivalent of the per capita income levels at which family income supplements were authorized. For 1988 and 1989 we rely on official estimates of the "subsistence minimum." These figures indicate that in 1975, 19.8 percent of the Soviet population lived below the poverty line. The rate of poverty fell to 17.9 percent in 1985. In 1988 and 1989, official estimates suggest a poverty rate in the range of 14.4 to 18.9 percent.

It is not clear whether any generally accepted estimates of subsistence minimums and poverty rates comparable to those shown in Table 3.1 for the late 1980s were issued by official agencies for 1990–91. But a fairly common view expressed in the domestic economic literature of the final two years of Soviet rule was that the poverty rate had increased to some 25–30 percent of the population.[5]

Whatever the actual rate, the continuing and wide-ranging discus-

Table 3.1

Official Soviet Estimates of Poverty Line and Proportion of Population Below Poverty Line (selected years, 1975–1989)

	1975	1985	1988	1989
Estimates of poverty line (rubles per capita per month)	50	75	78–84[a]	81–87[a]
Proportion of Soviet population below poverty line (in %)	19.8	17.9	14.5–18.6[b]	14.4–17.6[b]

Sources: Institute sotsial′no-ekonomikecheskikh problem narodonaseleniia, *Perestroika v sisteme raspretelitel′nykh otnoshenii* (Moscow, 1992), p. 80; V. Gur′ev and A. Zaitseva, "The Cost of Living, the Subsistence Minimum, Inflation (Methodology and Analysis)," *Vestnik statistiki,* 1990, no. 6, p. 26; Gosudarstvennyi komitet SSSR po statistiki, *Sotsial′noe razvitie SSSR 1989* (Moscow, 1991), p. 117. The figures on the proportion of the population below the poverty line in 1975 are our estimates based on material in Tsentral′noe statisticheskoe upravlenie pri Sovete Ministrov SSR, *Narodnoe khoziaistvo SSSR v 1974 g.* (Moscow, 1975), p. 35. The proportions below the poverty line in 1985 and 1989 are estimated from material in Gosudarstvennyi komitet SSSR, p. 117.

[a]The lower figure in this range is the subsistence minimum calculated on the basis of prices in state and cooperative retail outlets. The higher figure also takes account of prices in collective farm markets.

[b]Some Soviet sources cite 41 million people below the subsistence minimum in both 1988 and 1989. This would imply 14.4% and 14.3% of the population, respectively, in those two years. The range of figures we show here corresponds to the range of estimates of the poverty line and was calculated with the aid of data on income distribution in the sources cited above.

sions reveal the salience of the poverty issue in the period since the initiation of economic reforms early in 1992. It is also clear that there were serious difficulties in making comparisons between the kind of poverty data available for the pre-1992 period and more recent years. Some caveats follow.

In the first place, as we noted in Chapter 2, under Soviet communism the state provided a wide array of free social goods including universal health care, education, and vocational training. Subsidized housing, though mostly overcrowded, virtually eliminated homelessness. At the workplace, trade unions provided for a broad range of social services that included inexpensive recreation, vacations, and child care, which enabled women to work. While the state guaranteed everyone a job, control over employment and wages kept the level of average wages close to what families needed to cover the costs of basic necessities. Some essential consumer goods were heavily subsidized, keeping their prices low, but they were generally of poor quality and frequently in short supply. Most people accepted this low standard of living in exchange for economic and social security and a relatively equal distribution of available goods and services. The gradual improvement in living standards during the Brezhnev years provided some hope of a brighter future.[6]

It should also be clear that the poverty data reviewed thus far apply to the USSR as a whole, and not to the Russian Federation as such. Poverty in Russia was undoubtedly lower than in the USSR as a whole (assuming, of course, that the "poverty line" taken as applicable to the USSR was also roughly appropriate for Russia). Indeed, Soviet discussions of the poverty issue in the late 1980s and early 1990s commonly focused on the relatively high poverty rates in the Central Asian republics, Kazakhstan, and Azerbaijan, and linked the poverty problem with the large number of children commonly generated by families in these regions.[7] While the problems of the poor in other areas of the Soviet Union were not completely ignored, they were certainly treated as less pressing than in the Central Asian republics, where poverty rates in the late 1980s were in the range of 30–50 percent.

In contrast to the Central Asian republics, the poverty rate for the Russian Republic during this time was approximately 5 percent.[8] This estimate, derived by two British scholars, seems rather low but is the only available figure we have for Russia in 1989.* However, it must be kept in mind that most Russian families had incomes not much above the poverty line. When the problem of poverty in Russia was discussed, it was commonly linked to the fate of pensioners (especially "pure pensioners"—those forced to live apart from their families and dependent on pension income alone) and young families at an early stage in their work careers. Unlike the situation that would emerge in 1992–93, poverty in Russia in the late 1980s was not treated as a "mass phenomenon."

Another feature worth noting concerns the spending patterns of those groups commonly classified as poor at the end of the 1980s (and presumably in 1990–91 as well). A variety of sources indicate that food

---

*The subsistence income used to establish the poverty rate is based on a monthly per capita income of 75 rubles. In fact, the official subsistence minimum for the USSR was estimated at 81 to 88 rubles per month, depending on the prices used in the calculations.

accounted for approximately one-half of a poor family's total family expenditures during this period.[9] By 1992, official definitions of the poverty threshold assumed that outlays on food absorbed, on the average, more than two-thirds of the income of the poor. Any attempt to compare official poverty rates before and since 1992 must come to terms with these changing criteria for defining the poverty threshold.

Finally, one additional difference between the treatment of the poverty issue before and after liberalization should be recognized. It concerns the changing intellectual and political environment in which this subject has been discussed, in particular, the opportunities for "independent" assessments of the poverty problem. The material reviewed above on the subsistence minimum and poverty rates through the late 1980s was based on official or, at the very least, semi-official reports. By 1990 some Soviet publications began to carry alternative estimates of the poverty threshold issued by different state agencies, as well as (higher) estimates prepared by trade unions that had ceased to function as simply another arm of the state.[10] By 1993–94 a growing Russian literature questioning the methods used by official agencies to assess the poverty problem and presenting independent estimates of poverty rates had emerged. This evolution reflects not only the flowering of intellectual freedom, but also the emergence of a civil society in which differing assessments of the extent of poverty accompanying the market transition necessarily functioned as political weapons in the social and ideological conflicts of these years.

How Many Poor? The Rise of Mass Poverty

When official Russian estimates of the poverty threshold and the extent of poverty in 1992–93 began to emerge, it became clear that the methods and criteria used to derive these magnitudes were markedly different from those commonly used in earlier years. Whatever the scientific or technical grounds for these changes, they also served a political function—to keep official poverty rates within reasonable bounds. Reliance on earlier methods would almost certainly have implied that the economic reforms initiated at the beginning of 1992 had forced the overwhelming bulk of the Russian population into a state of poverty. There are a variety of ways of demonstrating the consequences and nature of these changes in deriving poverty rates.

Boris Yeltsin clearly recognized the increasing significance of the poverty problem as he moved toward implementing radical reforms. In an address to the Russian people at the end of October 1991, he summed up the difficult situation confronting the nation:

> The time has come for resolute, strict, unhesitating action. Everyone knows the starting base. The situation is tense. There are difficulties with food and with the primary necessities. The financial system is on the verge of collapsing. Inflation has reached the critical point. Fifty-five percent of all families live below the poverty line. The situation is not improving.
>
> . . . The one-time transition to market prices is a difficult, forced, but necessary measure . . . . Things will be worse for everyone for about half a year whereupon prices will drop and the consumer market will be filled with goods. But as I promised before the election, the economy will stabilize and the living standard will gradually improve by the autumn of 1992.[11]

Of course, none of these optimistic predictions was realized. Nevertheless, it must be assumed that Yeltsin's reference to 55 percent of families below the poverty line was not simply dreamed up to justify the onset of economic reforms, but reflected the findings of Russian state agencies entrusted with providing reasonable estimates of poverty rates. Given the widely acknowledged and substantial decline in real per capita income that ensued in 1992–93, one would expect poverty rates in this period to have increased significantly, especially if such rates continued to be calculated as they had been earlier. Indeed, an International Labor Organization (ILO) study published early in 1992 must have relied on poverty estimates that were in continuity with Yeltsin's 55 percent figure for the end of 1991 when it noted the following: "In early 1992 as many as 85 percent of the population were said to be living below the poverty line. . . ."[12] The implications of continuing to rely on pre-1992 methods of calculating the poverty threshold were formulated in even more extreme terms by a Russian economist, Marina Mozhina. Writing at about the same time, she warned: "If we take the previously accepted norm of the minimum consumer basket [used to calculate the subsistence minimum] and calculate it in today's free prices . . . the entire population will indeed be below the poverty line."[13]

To avoid the social policy and political implications of treating most Russians as poor, beginning in 1992, new procedures were devised to calculate a subsistence minimum below which an individual would be classified as poor. This "absolute" measure of poverty was developed by estimating the value of a basket of food that guaranteed a sufficient number of calories and whose composition conformed to Russian tastes and the recommendations of the international health (World Health Organization—WHO) and food (Food and Agriculture Organization—FAO) organizations. The food component of the budget was valued at current prices and then expanded to include nonfood items. It was assumed that on the average the poor spent 68 percent of their income on food. As we noted earlier, in the 1980s (and presumably in 1990–91 as well) outlays on food were assumed to absorb approximately one-half of a poor family's expenditures. Of course, as the economists Anthony Atkinson and John Micklewright note, "there can be no such thing as a single absolute poverty standard. Subsistence needs must in part reflect the standard of living of the country in which those needs are being assessed."[14] In raising the proportion of the income that the poor were estimated to have spent on food, the Ministry of Labor assumed that Russians had changed their consumption patterns as a result of sharply declining living standards.

Table 3.2 shows the expenditure patterns believed to prevail among various demographic groups classified as poor by the Russian Ministry of Labor beginning in 1992. The 68 percent figure for food outlays is certainly high by Western standards, but it is worth noting that some Russian economists thought it too low. Thus, Mozhina argued that 80 percent as the share of food in total family expenditures was a more appropriate guide to setting the poverty threshold. The official figures, in her view, resulted in an exaggerated poverty rate that would encourage the kind of income supplements that could only intensify the inflation problem.[15]

The major components of the actual "food basket" used by the Ministry of Labor in setting its minimum subsistence budgets since 1992 (i.e., food consumption corresponding to the poverty threshold) were also modified. Where comparisons can be made with the "food basket" used to derive the subsistence minimum in the late 1980s (for the Soviet Union as a whole rather than for the Russian Federation) some interesting differences emerge. Table 3.3 shows the minimum "food baskets" used by official agencies in the late 1980s and 1992 to derive the poverty line (and thus the poverty rate). The most obvious changes revealed in the food content of the subsistence minimum are

Table 3.2

Expenditure Patterns Assumed by Russian Ministry of Labor in Deriving Minimum Subsistence Budgets (Poverty Lines) of Various Demographic Groups, 1992–1994 (%)

Expenditure items	Population as a whole (per capita)	Distribution of expenditures (in %) for the following groups:		Children	
		Working-age population	Pensioners	Age 0–6	Age 7–15
Food	68.3	61.6	82.9	74.5	73.4
Nonfood products	19.1	21.4	10.0	18.9	19.8
Services	7.4	8.9	7.1	6.6	6.8
Taxes and other payments	5.2	8.1	—	—	—
Total expenditures	100.0	100.0	100.0	100.0	100.0

Source: Rossiiskie vesti, April 21, 1994, p. 1.

Table 3.3

Minimum "Food Baskets" Used by Official Agencies to Derive Minimum Subsistence Budgets, Late 1980s (USSR) and 1992 (Russia)
(in kilograms per capita, per year)

Food items	Late 1980s[a]	1992
Bread products	97	129.6
Potatoes	89	124.8
Vegetables	110[b]	93.6
Sugar and confectionary products	25	20.4
Fruits and berries	65	19.2
Fish products	18	10.8
Meat products	54	26.4
Milk products	331	211.2
Eggs[c]	234	151.2
Oil and margarine	10[d]	9.6

Sources: V.G. Gur'ev and A. Zaitseva, "The Cost of Living, the Subsistence Minimum, and Inflation (Methodology and Analysis)," *Vestnik statistiki,* 1990, no. 6, p. 20; G. Valiuzhenik, "The Survival Threshold," *Argumenty i fakty,* 1993, no. 4, p. 3.

[a]The source on which we rely here does not make clear whether these figures apply to 1988 or 1989 or both.

[b]This figure applies to vegetables and melons.

[c]These figures apply to number of eggs.

[d]This figure applies to oil.

those that might be expected to take place during a period of declining living standards—increased dependence on bread and potatoes, and reduced consumption of fruits, vegetables, meats, and dairy products. An OECD study notes that such changes in food consumption reflect a pattern of behavior usually following "the impoverishment of the majority of the population."[16]

The subsistence budget allowed for less than one-third of personal income for nonfood items. This was clearly inadequate. As prices for nonfood products soared between 1992 and 1995, the poor were unable to purchase most of these goods. The absence of warm clothing and medicine was especially troublesome. In addition, the marketization of housing and public utilities had increased the share of rent, electricity, and telephone service from 3–5 percent to 10–20 percent of an average family budget.[17] Rising relative prices for clothing, consumer durables, housing, utilities, transportation, and other services meant that less could be spent on food. Consequently, in 1995 the Ministry of Labor revised the share of food in the subsistence budget from 68.3 percent to 57 percent.

When the principal features of the new subsistence minimum (as shown in Tables 3.2 and 3.3) were initially publicly announced, a spokesman for the Ministry of Labor stressed its temporary nature: "I repeat, this subsistence minimum is intended for a short, crisis period of time. Its norms and its composition will be changed in the future."[18] Despite the recent revisions, the essential structure and composition of this subsistence minimum have not changed very much.[19] Nor has there been any particular effort to conceal the fact that the definition of the poverty threshold was originally altered to reflect the general decline in living standards that accompanied the Yeltsin government's economic reforms. Thus, a Ministry of Labor spokesman noted that if the "earlier" (pre-1992) method of calculating the subsistence minimum (the "minimum consumption budget") had remained in effect, the ruble value of the poverty line at the end of 1992 would have been more than double the new officially announced figure.[20]

The view that recent Russian methods of calculating poverty reflect local circumstances—and rightly so—rather than anything approximating "universal" criteria of poverty was also clearly implied in a comment by economists associated with a research group headed by Egor Gaidar. In a review of the performance of the Russian economy in 1993, they noted the following: "Every third Russian has an income below the subsistence minimum (if the definition of poverty accepted in the USA had been used, 60 percent of families would be below the poverty line)."[21]

Despite the acknowledged limitations of the Ministry of Labor's measure of poverty, what has been the trend in the government's estimates of the rate of poverty? As Table 3.4 shows, in the year following liberalization, more than one-third of all Russians were classified as poor. The poverty rate declined between 1992 and 1993 from approximately 36 percent to 29 percent, dropped to 25 percent in 1994, but increased again to 29 percent in 1995. The number of poor began to decline again in the first half of 1996, falling to approximately 24 percent of the population. While such figures were well below the poverty rate invoked by President Yeltsin in 1991, they were still approximately five times higher than its pre-reform level. Moreover, the findings of nonofficial studies indicated that poverty had spread to engulf a much broader group of Russians. These new studies confirmed what most Russians already knew: poverty had become a mass phenomenon.

Table 3.4

Subsistence Minimum and Percentage of Population in Russia Below Poverty Level, 1992–1996

	Income per capita corresponding to subsistence minimum (rubles per month)	Percentage of population below poverty level
1992	1,900	36
1993	20,578	29
1994	86,564	25
1995	264,100	29
1996		
January	345,500	25
February	357,400	25
March	365,500	24

Source: Ministry of Labor estimates. Working Center for Economic Reform, Government of the Russian Federation, *Russian Economic Trends*, 1996, vol. 5, no. 1, pp. 56–57.

Alternative Estimates of Poverty

Soon after the government published its estimates of the incidence of poverty, alternative measures of poverty appeared. Developed by respected social scientists, these studies served as explicit or implicit criticisms of the government's method of estimating the incidence of poverty. In some cases, the criticism was directed at the methods used to calculate the subsistence minimum budget that serves as the basis for deriving the official poverty rates. In other cases, the critique was implicit in the different estimates of poverty that emerged. The results of these investigations imply that the official statistics significantly underestimated the severity of the poverty problem.

If these critical responses were simply the reactions of political opponents of the government obviously aimed at exaggerating the poverty problem, they would deserve only passing attention. But as will be apparent, some of the critics (judging by their reputations) are probably at least as "scientifically" oriented as the scholars who derived the official estimates. Since alternative methods were used, we make no attempt to adjust the official figures to take into account the analysis of the alternative measures of poverty. At best, it might be useful to view

Table 3.5

Nonofficial Estimates of Russian Poverty Rates

Sources of estimates	Period	Estimated proportion of impoverished population (%)
All-Russian Standard of Living Center	First half of 1994	39 ("poor")
Argumenty i fakty	January–April 1994	27–28 ("poor") 33–34 ("extremely poor")
Russian Center for Public Opinion Research (VTsIOM)	March 1994	50–58 ("poor")
Tat'iana I. Zaslavskaia	June–December 1993	31.1 ("poor") 9.6 ("extremely poor")

Sources: V. Bobkov and P. Maslovskii-Mstislavskii, "Incomes Policy: Wages, Taxes, Savings," *Izvestiia*, October 19, 1994; Noi Khubulova, "The Rich and the Poor," *Argumenty i fakty*, 1994, no. 24; L. Zubova, N. Kovaleva, and L. Khakhulina, "Poverty Under New Economic Conditions," *Ekonomicheskie i sotsial'nye peremeny: Monitoring obshchestvennogo mneniia*, 1994, no. 4, p. 25; T.I. Zaslavskaia, "Real Incomes of Russians Through the Prism of Social Assessments," *Obshchestvo i ekonomika*, 1994, nos. 3–4, pp. 61–62.

the official rates shown in Table 3.4 as the lower limit of a range of probable poverty rates.

Table 3.5 presents alternative estimates of the extent of poverty by a number of nonofficial (or, at most, semi-official) sources. The comparatively "respectable" nature of these sources and their consistently higher estimates of poverty rates are worth noting. Thus, the highest estimate (60–62 percent), based on the combined sum of the "poor" and "extremely poor" *(nishchie)*, appeared in the weekly *Argumenty i fakty*, generally considered to be supportive of the Yeltsin government. The poverty rate for the first half of 1994 suggested by the All-Russian Standard of Living Center was 39 percent, compared with a rate of approximately 25 percent claimed by its official parent organization, the Ministry of Labor.

Researchers at the Russian Center for Public Opinion Research (VTsIOM) developed an alternative measure of poverty that is based on "relative" rather "absolute" standards for determining the poverty line. As noted earlier, absolute measures of poverty establish a poverty threshold based on an estimated fixed and irreducible subsistence standard. In the VTsIOM approach, the poor included those members of the Russian population whose income was no more than one-half of the average per capita income in the country as a whole.[22] This meant establishing a poverty threshold of 70 thousand rubles per month per capita instead of the "official" subsistence minimum of 60.4 thousand rubles. In such a measure of relative poverty (commonly used in the European community), the poverty line is linked to changes in average income. If average per capita income falls and the decline is distributed equally, then the proportion of the population that is relatively poor will not change. But if average per capita income falls and the decline is unequally shared, then the rate of poverty will increase. In the Russian case, average income fell at the same time that the distribution of income widened sharply. As a result, relative poverty increased dramatically. Using this method, VTsIOM calculated a poverty rate in the neighborhood of 50 percent for early 1994, approximately twice the official rate. It is clear from their analysis that growing inequality was becoming the major source of increasing poverty.

Tat'iana Zaslavskaia developed another measure of poverty based on the population's subjective assessment of the "subsistence minimum." She asked respondents to estimate what they considered to be the minimum income necessary to meet basic needs. She then compared those assessments with the respondents' actual income to determine the proportion of the population that fell below what she calls the "social subsistence minimum." Unlike the other estimates shown in Table 3.5, Zaslavskaia's figure applies to the second half of 1993. But like the other nonofficial poverty rate figures, it is distinctly higher than the official reports on the extent of poverty for the comparable period (41 percent versus 28 to 34 percent). In any case, it should be clear now why we suggested earlier that the official poverty estimates should be regarded—at best—as the lower limit of a reasonable range of poverty rates whose upper limit may have approached one-half of the Russian population during much of 1992–94.

The New Poor: The Poverty of the Strong

Thus far, we have been primarily concerned with examining the increasing incidence of poverty in Russia since the onset of radical economic reforms. We now turn our attention more closely to the groups most likely to be found among the poor, and ask whether the face of poverty has changed since the collapse of communism.

In some respects, the answer given by government agencies to this question is no different from answers that might have been offered in the final years of Soviet rule. Thus, a number of sources make it clear that, as in the past, families with many children (where "many" usually means three or more) and single-parent households are among the most vulnerable groups. Between one-half and three-quarters of such units were apparently below the poverty line in 1992–93.[23] This helps explain why approximately 40 percent or more of all children in Russia up to the age of fifteen were being raised in households below the official poverty threshold during this period.[24]

But despite such continuities with the past, the face of poverty in Russia has changed. Poverty not only afflicts the weak, but increasingly strikes employed wage-earners and has unexpectedly also touched better-educated professionals and skilled workers. In Russia today, low wages are a more significant determinant of poverty than the number of dependents in a household. In the early 1990s, the breadwinner had a regular job in about two-thirds of poor households.[25]

During the Soviet era it was extremely unlikely that a family with two workers would become poor. Since most women worked, most households had two wage-earners. Therefore, as we noted above, the groups especially at risk were single-parent families or large families, as well as young households with a wife on maternity leave. Social benefits such as maternity and child–care allowances, disability pensions, and assistance to single-parent and large families were targeted to help these vulnerable groups. For most young families poverty was only temporary and often alleviated with parental support. Once both spouses resumed work—facilitated by the provision of preschool child care—the risk of remaining in poverty ended.

This is no longer true in post-Soviet Russia. Employment is no guarantee that a family will escape poverty. While the two-income family, a legacy of Soviet policy, provides an important buffer against declining real income, it no longer is an escape from falling into poverty. A family with one or two children with both spouses working is now the most numerous category of the poor, representing in 1993 40 percent of the population below the poverty line.[26]

Clearly what has happened is the emergence of a "new poor" and new sources of social and economic inequality. While the more tradi-

Table 3.6

Occupational Composition of Main Breadwinners in Working Families, March 1994: Study Conducted by Russian Center for Public Opinion Research (VTsIOM)(%)

Occupational status	All working families	All poor working families	25% poorest working families
Managerial personnel	9	6	5
Specialists	23	21	16
White-collar employees	15	12	13
Skilled workers	43	50	52
Unskilled workers	10	11	15
Total	100	100	101

Source: L. Zubova et al., "Poverty Under New Economic Conditions," p. 26.

tional poor have certainly not been ignored in recent discussions, the poverty problem is increasingly seen as linked to the relatively low real incomes of full-time workers in the old "productive" sectors and of selected groups of white-collar employees with advanced education, as well as the growing number of unemployed. We examine these problems more fully in Chapter 5. As for the broad issue of inequality between the lower and upper levels of the economic ladder, it cannot be adequately discussed without invoking categories that would have appeared alien in the Russian setting a few years earlier— property income versus wage income, private sector versus state sector employment.

Some independent scholars and research groups have looked more closely at these new dimensions of poverty and inequality. For example, VTsIOM researchers found that in the mid-1990s, 70 percent of the main breadwinners in a representative sample of working poor they surveyed were skilled workers or "specialists" (presumably mainly engineering-technical personnel), with the great bulk of these being employed in the state sector (see Table 3.6). These were obviously groups that could have been reasonably regarded as largely "middle-income strata" in the Soviet era.[27] The essential message of this study was that the phenomenon of mass impoverishment was not primarily a problem of large family size or the plight of suddenly impoverished pensioners, but reflected a decline in the real income of broad sections

Table 3.7

Proportion of Various Socio-Occupational Groups Classified as "Poor" and "Extremely Poor" in Zaslavskaia's Studies of Graduations of Economic Status, May–November 1993

Socio-occupational groups[a]	% of groups falling into the following categories:		
	Extremely poor[b]	Poor	Total
Workers' elite	—	3	3
Intellectual elite	—	6	6
Higher-level managers	7	16	23
State administration	7	30	37
Mass intelligentsia	9	40	49
Office personnel	14	40	54
Skilled workers	10	42	52
Peasants	21	40	61
Unskilled workers	18	43	61
All groups	10	32	42

Source: Tat'iana Zaslavskaia, "Real Incomes of Russians Through the Prism of Social Assessments," *Obshchestvo i ekonomika*, 1994, nos. 3–4, pp. 71–72.

[a]Our source indicates that these groups are listed in order of their declining income. If this is intended to be the case, one must wonder why office personnel (characterized as generally "without specialized education") are shown above skilled workers.

[b]This included individuals whose monthly income was less than one-half of the lower range of the subsistence minimum.

of the wage-earning population and the growth of (both open and concealed) unemployment.

Other VTsIOM studies of the composition of the impoverished population were conducted by the sociologist Tat'iana Zaslavskaia. We referred earlier to her reliance on public perceptions of the subsistence minimum and "normal" incomes as guidelines for setting the poverty threshold as well as higher gradations of economic status. Such perceptions, together with data on the nominal incomes of samples of the employed population, were used to estimate the proportion of the country's population living in poverty, as well as the proportion of particular socio-occupational groups in this position.

Zaslavskaia's estimates of the extent of impoverishment (the sum total of the proportions classified as "extremely poor" and "poor") among various socio-occupational groups are shown in Table 3.7. Of special interest is the relatively high poverty rate (49 percent) among the "mass intelligentsia" stratum. While the precise occupational groups included in this category are not spelled out fully, they include such groups as physicians, teachers, journalists, and engineering-technical personnel. No less important is Zaslavskaia's designation of more than one-half of skilled workers (the category entitled "basic stratum of workers") as either "poor" (42 percent) or "extremely poor" (10 percent). The fall of many of the former Soviet middle strata into poverty helps explain why inequality has grown so sharply. As poverty spread to include a wider range of occupations, a larger proportion of the population was now bunched around the poverty line while a few had moved up the income ladder. The result is a thinning of the income distribution at the top.

A few additional features of Zaslavskaia's findings are worth noting. The socio-occupational groups shown in Table 3.7 appear in order of their declining money and real incomes (from highest to lowest), based on their *admitted* incomes.[28] It may seem strange that groups characterized as worker elites and intellectual elites should have higher incomes and lower poverty rates than higher-level managerial personnel (as implied by Table 3.7). Indeed, notes Zaslavskaia, this distorts the real situation. "There is no doubt that . . . the actual level of living of higher level managerial personnel is higher than that of the worker and intellectual elites."[29] The data in Table 3.7 simply fail to record a series of privileges available to plant directors and their close associates—essentially preferential access to high-quality housing space, building materials, consumer goods, auto transport, and other amenities.

With the exception of the peasants' category, the socio-occupational strata shown in Table 3.7 may be characterized as wage-earning groups. More than two-fifths of all wage-earners *(rabotaiushchie po naimu)* in Zaslavskaia's study fell below the poverty threshold (33 percent were classified as "poor" and 10 percent as "extremely poor"). It hardly comes as a surprise that the poverty rates for Zaslavskaia's sample of "employers" or "entrepreneurs" *(predprinimateli)* were substantially below this level. But like the wage-earners' category, the employers' category was a rather heterogeneous one. None of those characterized as "owners of enterprises" fell below the poverty line, while the poverty rate for the "self-employed" was only 1 percent. However, for those in the employers' category who sought to combine work in wage-earning occupations with involvement in their own business ("semi-entrepreneurs"—*polupredprinimateli*) the poverty rate was 21 percent.[30] While these differences in poverty rates are hardly unexpected, they clearly highlight—once again—the emergence of new sources of inequality associated with radical changes in the system of property ownership, a process reflected most clearly in the sharply contrasting poverty rates of wage-earners and "owners of enterprises,"[31] and a growing divide between the new poor and the new rich.

We conclude by pointing to one additional source of differential Russian poverty rates that reflects broader patterns of social and economic inequality in the society as a whole. Little attention is generally paid in Russian discussions of the poverty problem to those of its aspects that reflect gender inequalities. Zaslavskaia's study is one of the few that at least touches on this relationship. Thus, 71 percent of the employed "extremely poor" and 67 percent of the employed "poor" in her study were women. As might be expected, the proportion of positions at the other end of the economic spectrum (classified by Zaslavskaia as "well-to-do" and "prosperous") filled by men was approximately of the same order of magnitude as the proportion of positions at the bottom filled by women. But in Zaslavskaia's view, the resulting situation represented more than simply a continuation of the past. "The difference in the material position of men and women, which has always been quite appreciable, has now become shocking."[32] We discuss this issue more fully and examine some of the empirical grounds for this generalization in the next chapter.

The emergence of "mass impoverishment" and the "new poor" suggests the urgency of revising the radical economic strategy. Just before the June 1996 presidential election, the International Monetary Fund—a strong advocate of conservative monetary and fiscal policy—began to modify its position on Russian economic reform. As one of the IMF officials acknowledged, the management of the Russian economy will not succeed unless the problems of the poor are more adequately addressed.[33]

The growing incidence of poverty in Russia has provoked new concerns about the problems of the poor. Some critics are questioning whether Russia is creating an underclass similar to those that exist in many Latin American countries. Clear differences between the poor in less developed economies and in Russia are, of course, still evident. As Branko Milanovic suggests in his recent study of poverty in Russia and Eastern Europe, the poor in these countries still possess relatively high educational levels, reasonable housing and household assets, and still have access to social services and health care not available to the extremely poor in less developed economies. Moreover, the spread of poverty in Russia is still relatively recent, and the average income of the Latin American poor is much more significantly below the poverty line than that of the average Russian poor.[34]

Nevertheless, some apprehension may be called for. If it takes too much longer for Russia to emerge from its profound economic depression, the welfare of the poor will continue to deteriorate and a significant percentage of Russia's young people will not have escaped the social deprivation associated with poverty. Nor is the resumption of economic growth by itself a solution to the problems of the poor. As we have suggested, one of the major causes of poverty in Russia has been the growth in inequality. Therefore, social and economic policies to reduce income inequality and to repair the broken social safety net are also necessary.

The symptoms of extreme poverty are already visible in Russia's largest cities. According to one estimate, there are now 60,000 homeless children in Moscow.[35] They have been augmented since 1992 by the 4 million migrants and refugees caused by the disintegration of the Soviet Union. In Moscow, Mayor Yuri Luzhkov, supported by President Yeltsin, has begun deporting thousands of homeless people. As one of the mayor's legal advisers, Aleksandr Zolin, argued, "we're not saying there should be an iron curtain separating Moscow from the rest of the country, but we don't need homeless vagrants or beggars here." In denying political rights to the homeless, Zolin advocated a new Russian concept of freedom: "If people can afford to live here," he argued, "they are welcome, if they cannot they should stay where they are. In our view, there is no freedom without financial means."[36] According to official statistics, as many as 45 million Russians were poor at the beginning of 1995.[37] If Russia implements this concept of freedom, the liberty of millions would once again be at risk.

4

A Question of Difference:
Women as Losers

Soon after seizing power in 1917 the Bolsheviks abolished all previous laws that restricted women's rights. Along with introducing the principle of equal pay for equal work, a special decree proclaimed marriage to be voluntary, giving each partner equal parental and property rights. All subsequent Soviet constitutions contained special articles proclaiming the equality of the sexes in all spheres of life.

But these measures did not ensure that women were equal in practice. The Soviet Union gave women legal equality at work as well as in the home, but women's equality in both places was undermined by their treatment as secondary members of the labor force and by traditional perceptions of women's roles at home. After the fall of communism, when the market began to regulate the decisions of all workers, women tended to lose some of these formal protections in the workplace without gaining the support services at home that would enable them to compete effectively in a "free market" environment. The consequences left women more vulnerable both in the labor market and in their unpaid roles in the home.

While the pre-perestroika discussions on the position of women in Soviet society frequently celebrated socialist "achievements" in the area of equality of the sexes, it was always clear that the "emancipation" of women had not been achieved. A considerable amount of Soviet literature documented the relatively disadvantaged position of women as reflected in their earnings, occupational status, and responsibility for household chores. Western scholars had abundant Soviet source material to draw on that pointed out the continued subordinate economic and social status of Soviet women.[1]

The persistence of gender inequality can be traced to a basic contradiction in Soviet ideology and policies. On the one hand, Soviet communism promoted women's full participation in the workplace as a precondition for achieving social and political as well as economic equality. On the other hand, it was assumed that household work and child rearing were primarily a woman's responsibility. These conflicting objectives inevitably undermined women's workforce roles. The goal of equal opportunity for men and women remained elusive.

Yet the Soviet Union did successfully bring women into the workforce.* The labor force participation rate of Soviet women in the late 1980s was among the highest in the world—if not the highest. According to the 1989 population census, 84.1 percent of working-age women in the Russian Republic were employed (approximately the same proportion as in 1979 and 1970). In addition, about 7 percent were regarded as full-time students. Thus, less than one-tenth of working-age women could be regarded as available for full-time engagement as "housewives" and in child-rearing activities.[2] In 1991, women outnumbered men in the workforce by 52 percent to 48 percent, a decline from even higher levels.[3] Yet, despite their exceptionally high level of labor force participation, time-budget studies undertaken during the Soviet period confirmed that women performed the bulk of household work.[4]

In seeking to reduce women's "double burden" and protect their maternal functions, Soviet law treated women differently from men. An array of social and labor legislation restricted women's employment and provided special concessions to enable them to combine full-time employment with family responsibilities. These concessions included maternity benefits, child-care leaves, day care, summer camps, lighter work loads, and shorter work periods as well as protective labor laws that regulated women's labor. Regulations prohibited

---

*The ideological commitment to bring women into the workforce was reinforced by economic necessity. In the 1930s, many women joined the workforce as a result of the declining real incomes of their husbands. On the demand side, state enterprises needed to employ more women to meet their output goals as Soviet planning increasingly depended on the mobilization of labor to increase economic growth. After World War II, the need for women's labor intensified because of the sharp decline in the availability of male workers.

night-shift work and contained restrictions on lifting and carrying heavy loads and working under dangerous conditions. They also provided special compensations such as wage supplements, shorter work periods, additional leave, and early retirement for women working in activities that did not comply with the norms and regulations of labor protection.[5]

As the Russian economy stumbled toward a market system, women discovered that special laws protecting their ability to fulfill family roles while fully employed undermined their ability to compete in the new labor market. In 1990–91, a series of decrees aimed at enhancing pregnancy leaves, providing absentee days to care for children, and the right to work part-time or on a more flexible schedule provided additional concessions for working parents. In practice, they were directed primarily at women. But the decrees raised questions. Why should employers hire a woman if they must pay additional costs to cover benefits available only to women? What should women do? Should they give up the tensions of their "double day" and return to the home and the promise of a husband to support them and their children? Could they afford to do so? And what about the personal consequences of giving up their economic independence? Why should women bear the major burden of child rearing and family responsibilities?

As Ulla Wikander, Alice Kessler-Harris, and Jane Lewis observe in Protecting Women, "these questions capture the central tension around women's efforts to juggle family and work responsibilities in the modern world." They are central to Soviet and post-Soviet efforts of "pitting the demand for equality in the workplace against the well-intentioned efforts of men and women to protect family life."[6] They are at the heart of what feminists have identified as the difference/equality question.

In his vision of perestroika, Mikhail Gorbachev outlined how a reformed Soviet Union would address "the women's question":

> [D]uring our difficult and heroic history, we failed to pay attention to women's specific rights and needs arising from their role as mother and homemaker, and their indispensable educational function as regards children. Engaged in scientific research, working on construction sites, in industry and the service sector, and involved in creative activities, women no longer have enough time to perform their everyday duties at home—housework, raising children and the creation of a good family

atmosphere. We have discovered that many of our problems—in children's and young people's behavior, in our morals, culture and even industry—are partially caused by the weakening of family ties and a slack attitude to family responsibilities. This is a paradoxical result of our sincere and politically justified desire to make women equal with men in everything.[7]

In proposing solutions to women's double burden, Gorbachev rejected the classical socialist assumption that "without the full and equal participation of women in social production, their genuine equality with men was inconceivable," and accepted a reduced role for women in the workplace. "Now in the course of *perestroika*," he writes, "we have begun to overcome this shortcoming. That is why we are now holding debates in the press, in public organizations, at work and at home, about the question of what we should do to make it possible for *women to return to their purely womanly mission*" (our emphasis).[8]

Gorbachev's response may have reflected the anticipated need to reduce employment as the Soviet Union entered a period of radical economic reform. Women were a natural target. In the past, other voices had called for women's reduced role in the workforce. For example, natalists concerned with falling birth rates had clamored for more protection for mothers. In the final years of the Soviet Union, Gorbachev's gesture for women to have greater opportunities to pursue their maternal interests mirrored the initial transition from a planned economy based on labor shortages to a market economy characterized by a more open surplus of labor. As the perceived need for women workers diminished, even the formal commitment to women's full participation in the workplace crumbled.

Gender Inequalities: The Final Years of Soviet Rule

Faced with the extremely difficult task of combining full-time employment with primary responsibility for household labor, women have tended to adjust their work expectations, accepting lower-skilled jobs and wages in exchange for certain nonmonetary benefits such as shorter travel time to work, convenient hours, lighter work loads, easier access to shopping, and child-care facilities in their workplaces. As a consequence, women were more likely to be crowded into jobs well below their educational qualifications. In effect, women paid for the concessions and services they received in the form of lower wages.

Protective labor legislation also served to channel women into particular sectors and industrial branches of the economy. Despite images of Soviet women working in what most Americans would consider nontraditional jobs,* sexual stereotyping and prejudice persisted until the final years of the Soviet Union. Consequently, while there were relatively few women employed in heavy industry, mining, and construction, they were overrepresented in services and light industry. Teachers, doctors, scientific and cultural employees as well as textile, clothing, shoe, food, and clerical workers were mostly women. The crowding of women into particular sectors and jobs was the most significant factor responsible for the continued disadvantaged economic status of women in the final years of the Soviet Union and, in some instances, its deterioration.

Women's wages clearly reveal the perpetuation of this inequality. One of the methods commonly used to assess changes in the relative economic status of employed women has been to compare changes in earnings in selected "women's branches"—sectors in which women employees predominate—with trends in earnings in the economy or industry as a whole. This is hardly adequate as a measure of changing gender inequalities, but given the scarcity of data directly comparing men's and women's earnings over time, it has served as a kind of symbolic substitute. The results for the period 1986–89 (see Table 4.1, which applies to the Russian Republic) hardly suggested any progress toward closing the gender gap. Indeed, the opposite was the case. Earnings in sectors like health care and public education (in which women accounted for 75 percent to 80 percent of the total employment) all exhibited slower growth than average earnings in the economy as a whole.[9]

Scattered evidence on the average earnings of men and women in industry during the last ten to twelve years of Soviet rule also fails to reveal any signs of reduced gender differentials. Thus, the average earnings of women in Soviet industry in the late 1970s were commonly reported in Soviet sources as being 70 percent of men's earnings.[10] On the eve of the dissolution of the former Soviet Union in 1991, average earnings of women in Russian industry were reported to be 68 percent of those of men.[11] The differing territorial coverage of these indicators

---

*Employment restrictions meant to protect women's health did not prevent women from choosing hazardous and heavy work in order to fulfill their family responsibilities.

Table 4.1

Earnings in Selected "Women's Branches" as Percentage of Average Earnings in Economy as a Whole, Russian Republic, 1986, 1989

Sector	Earnings in sector as % of average earnings in economy as a whole		Women as % of total employment in sector, 1990
	1986	1989	
Health care, physical culture, social security	69.1	68.8	83
Public education	77.7	71.0	79
Culture	59.9	56.0	75
Art	75.6	68.3	55

Sources: First two columns are calculated from material in Statisticheskie komitet sodruzhestva nezavisimykh gosudarstv, *Strany-chleny SNG, Statisticheskii ezhegodnik* (Moscow, 1992), pp. 361–362; the last column is drawn from Institute ekonomiki RAN, *Rabotaiushchie zhenshchiny v uslovliakh perekhoda Rossii k rynku* (Moscow, 1993), p. 25.

obviously limits their significance, but the figures certainly provide no evidence that the reforms undertaken in the final years of the Soviet Union functioned to reduce gender inequalities in earnings. If anything, they point in the opposite direction. Gender wage differentials at this time continued to reflect the long-standing segmentation of women into relatively low-wage sectors of the economy.

In March 1989, the Soviet government's principal statistical agency undertook a sample survey designed to compare the distribution of men's and women's earnings. Some of the principal findings of this study are shown in Tables 4.2 and 4.3. It can hardly come as a surprise that for the sample as a whole, as well as for groups with identical levels of schooling, the proportion of men with relatively high wage levels was substantially greater than the proportion of women in these wage categories. A simple exercise based on the material in Table 4.3 reveals a situation that must have been particularly disturbing to women with career aspirations. Suppose we accept—somewhat arbitrarily—a wage of more than 250 rubles per month in March 1989 as signifying a relatively "high" or "adequate" wage level (average monthly earnings in the economy as a whole were 220 rubles in 1988 and 240 rubles in 1989). It then appears that men with no more than a primary or secondary school education were more likely to receive "adequate" or "high" wages than women with a higher education.

Table 4.2

Distribution of Soviet Male and Female Workers and Employees by Wage Level, March 1989 (%)

Wage level (in rubles)	Whole sample	Men	Women
Less than 80	2.8	1.6	4.1
80–90	4.9	2.1	7.8
91–100	3.8	2.0	5.7
101–120	8.8	5.0	12.8
121–140	8.7	5.7	11.9
141–160	10.4	8.3	12.5
161–180	10.2	9.7	10.7
181–200	9.3	10.1	8.5
201–220	6.9	7.8	5.9
221–250	9.5	11.9	7.1
251–300	10.6	14.2	6.7
301–350	5.6	8.1	3.0
351–400	3.3	5.0	1.5
More than 400	5.2	8.5	1.8
Total	100.0	100.0	100.0

Source: Gosudarstvennyi komitet SSSR po statistike, *Sotsial'noe razvitie SSSR 1989* (Moscow, 1991), p. 94.

Note: This survey was based on a sample of 310,000 families. It included only workers and employees who worked the whole month of March 1989.

Responses to the "Woman Question"

The issue of gender inequality appears to have been taken rather seriously by the Soviet government and its statistical agencies in 1988–89. The information released at the 19th Party Conference and the studies initiated in those years confirm official recognition of the existence of highly unequal opportunities for the professional advancement of men and women with similar levels of education. Such discrepancies between education and occupational opportunities presented in reports at the 19th Party Conference (held during the summer of 1988) suggest that almost one-half (48 percent) of men with higher or secondary specialized education held some form of managerial position *(rukovodiashchaia rabota)*. The comparable figure for women with similar levels of education was only 7 percent.[12]

To stimulate more open discussions about the "woman question,"

Table 4.3

Distribution of Soviet Workers and Employees, Male and Female, by Wage Level (March 1989) and Level of Education (%)

Wage level (in rubles)	Higher	Secondary specialized	Secondary	Incomplete secondary	Primary
Men					
Less than 80	0.3	1.0	2.0	2.4	3.8
80–90	0.4	1.8	2.5	2.6	4.1
91–100	0.5	1.8	2.4	2.3	3.3
101–120	2.1	4.8	5.8	5.8	7.4
121–140	4.0	5.6	5.9	6.2	7.4
141–160	6.2	8.7	8.7	8.5	9.5
161–180	8.8	10.3	9.4	9.9	11.2
181–200	10.1	10.8	10.0	9.8	9.6
201–220	8.3	7.9	7.6	7.6	8.0
221–250	13.8	12.1	11.3	11.4	10.2
251–300	18.0	13.7	13.3	13.4	10.9
301–350	10.3	7.8	7.9	7.9	6.4
351–400	6.6	4.9	4.8	4.5	3.4
Above 400	10.6	8.8	8.4	7.7	4.8
Total	100.0	100.0	100.0	100.0	100.0
Women					
Less than 80	0.8	2.0	5.6	7.0	10.8
80–90	1.2	6.8	10.2	10.2	14.4
91–100	1.5	5.9	6.9	6.6	8.4
101–120	5.6	14.6	14.2	12.9	13.6
121–140	9.6	14.0	11.8	10.3	10.0
141–160	13.1	14.1	11.6	10.6	9.7
161–180	13.8	11.2	9.7	9.1	8.3
181–200	12.0	8.5	7.5	7.4	5.9
201–220	8.7	5.7	5.3	5.4	4.4
221–250	11.3	6.2	6.2	7.1	4.9
251–300	11.4	5.5	5.9	6.9	5.0
301–350	5.1	2.6	2.6	3.2	2.2
351–400	2.5	1.3	1.2	1.6	1.2
Above 400	3.4	1.6	1.3	1.7	1.2
Total	100.0	100.0	100.0	100.0	100.0

Source: Gosudarstvennyi komitet SSSR po statistike, *Sotsial'noe razvitie SSSR 1989* (Moscow, 1991), p. 96.

the government created a national women's organization to link the Soviet Women's Committee to a national network of local women's councils.[13] But no less important in stimulating discussions of gender issues was the increasing evidence that women's relative economic position had failed to improve, and had probably deteriorated.

The years of glasnost and the early post-Soviet period witnessed the emergence of a much more critical discussion on the status of women than had appeared earlier, as well as a considerable diversity of views on the principal problems of women in Soviet, and then in Russian, society. A new group of Russian feminists challenged Gorbachev's view of the "woman question." Rather than supporting Gorbachev's appeal for women to resume their "maternal functions," they asked why Soviet women, despite achieving high levels of labor force participation, educational attainment, and political representation, continued to occupy secondary and subordinate social positions. And why were the unfolding market reforms further undermining the economic and social position of women?

Women were divided about how to respond to the choices glasnost offered. For some, weary of the double day and the false promises of equality, Gorbachev's call for providing opportunities to return to the home struck a positive chord. But many women rejected the view that women should give up paid employment for full-time motherhood. By 1988 these conflicting orientations could be observed in the renewed discussion of the problems of women in Soviet society.

In an article in a leading Soviet economics journal, *EKO (Ekonomika i organizatsiia promyshlennogo proizvodstvo)*, Tat'iana Boldyreva put the different interests of women into a new perspective. Boldyreva noted that different groups of Soviet women—like women elsewhere—might readily have different dominant interests. Some were oriented primarily toward a professional life; others saw their legitimate roles as primarily or even exclusively that of wives and mothers; still others wanted to engage in a combination of these roles. But the critical point that followed from this fairly obvious listing of differences in women's conceptions of their principal roles was stated unambiguously: "We must not decide for them, but give them the possibility of making a choice."[14] As if to stress that she was not alone in this view, Boldyreva cited a study by "experts" at a Soviet research organization, which concluded that "conditions should be created in society that would enable women to choose any path depending on what they considered more important . . . professional growth, raising children, or a combination of the two."[15]

Such a formulation of women's rights may not strike Western readers as being particularly bold. But stressing the principle of freedom to choose was hardly a common theme in the Soviet context. Moreover, given the unusually high (by international standards) proportion of Soviet women in the labor force, and their concentration in low-skilled, low-wage occupations, Boldyreva's argument clearly implied that meaningful freedom of choice in this area was commonly absent.

But a new group of feminist scholars associated with the Institute of Socioeconomic Problems of the Population questioned this way of formulating the problem. Their views were initially presented in a 1989 article in a journal still called *Kommunist* at the time (now *Svobodnaia mysl'*), and further developed in the literature of the final days of the Soviet regime and the early post-Soviet period.[16] Defining their position as explicitly egalitarian, they contended that offering women the freedom to choose had limited meaning unless real equality of opportunity existed. In their view, the freedom to choose had been undermined by the long-standing "patriarchal" nature of relations between the sexes. Indeed, the new feminists argued that the subordinate position of women had been reproduced and in some respects even reinforced "at the level of society as a whole." This was reflected in the "feminization" of the lower levels of the professional and occupational structure, the insignificant representation of women in organs of power, particularly at the higher level, and the preservation of the traditional division of labor in the household.[17] For much too long, they argued, Soviet authorities had relied on a single criterion of success in confronting the "women question"—the maximum possible involvement of women in the workforce. But absent any change in the sexual division of labor in the household, women faced the frequently noted "double burden," which in effect functioned to discredit the socialist project of the emancipation of women.

Although much of it involved a critique of the past, the new feminist perspective also argued *for* a certain position. While this point of view had a rather familiar quality, it also had—in some respects—a distinctly non-Marxian ring. The basic principle that guided the feminist position was "equality of social opportunity to realize one's individuality" independently of traditional gender stereotypes concerning the "natural" division of labor between men and women.[18] In similarly broad terms, feminists stressed the need "to expand the sphere of autonomy of the individual"—not only for women but for men as well. This meant essentially removing the barriers to participation in the "societal sphere" for women, and recognizing the legitimacy and normalcy of men assuming a larger range of functions in the household.

Whatever its broader implications, the feminist position obviously reflected the concerns of women for whom the limited opportunity for professional growth and decision-making authority at the workplace and in other areas of Soviet society was a principal grievance.

But when Boldyreva enunciated the principle "we must not decide for them," she also had in mind groups of women whose principal concerns were quite different from more career-oriented women. In her view, the findings of sociologists suggested that approximately 20–30 percent of women were oriented "only to the family"[19] (as distinct from those oriented primarily to work careers or to a combination of roles). For these women, the idea of making it economically possible to reduce women's participation in the labor force would be attractive. Put in somewhat different and perhaps more lofty terms, the implementation by women of their proper "social role" seemed to require some redistribution of female labor resources "in favor of housekeeping."[20] But how could women leave their jobs when family income had rapidly begun to fall?

Toward a Market Economy: Women as Losers

Whatever optimism feminists might have had during the initial stages of perestroika faded as the socioeconomic position of women deteriorated quickly with the onset of radical economic reform in 1992. Rapid inflation and declining employment opportunities eroded women's already low relative wages. Stabilization policies reduced the real value of social benefits women received in rearing children and managing the household. Decreased subsidies for a broad range of educational, cultural, and social services curtailed many benefits on which wage-earning women depended and undermined employment conditions in the principal women's branches. Moreover, having been largely excluded from political and economic power in the Soviet Union, women found themselves at a disadvantage while those who formerly held such power converted those influences into new wealth and property rights.

When in 1994 Tat´iana Zaslavskaia wrote that while differences in the economic status of men and women had always been "quite appreciable," they had now become "shocking," she was referring to her study of the demographic composition of various categories of employed persons, ranging from the "extremely poor" and "poor" at one

Table 4.4

Relative Share of Men and Women in Zaslavskaia's Categories of Economic Status of Employed Personnel, May–December 1993 (%)

Categories of economic status[a]	Men	Women	Total
Extremely poor	29	71	100
Poor	33	67	100
In need	45	55	100
In relatively comfortable circumstances	56	44	100
Well-to-do	68	32	100
Prosperous	73	27	100

Source: Tat'iana Zaslavskaia, "Real Incomes of Russians Through the Prism of Social Assessments," *Obshchestvo i ekonomika*, 1994, nos. 3–4, p. 73.

[a]These gradations are based on Zaslavskaia's reliance on public perceptions of "minimum subsistence" and "normal" income levels, as well as multiples of the latter, which were used as guidelines in distinguishing differences in the economic status of the employed population.

extreme to the "well-to-do" and "prosperous" at the other. Zaslavskaia's findings (based on surveys conducted during the second half of 1993) are shown in Table 4.4. They indicate that the lower the relative economic position of a group of employed personnel, the higher the relative share of women in this group. The higher the group's economic status, the greater the proportion of men in the group.[21] After nearly two years of market reform, women constituted the majority of the working poor and, of course, represented only a minority of the new rich.[22]

What accounts for the "gender asymmetry" of the ongoing market reform?[23] The evidence points to the continued crowding of women into low-income jobs and branches of the economy, and to the more limited employment opportunities for women. One recent study found that occupational segregation by gender rose steadily during the Soviet period and continued to increase during the early post-Soviet years.[24] Both feminists and their critics believe that the gendered distribution of jobs is the major factor contributing to the continued wage inequality between the sexes.

Unfortunately, the types of comparative surveys of men and women's earnings conducted by the Soviet Union's principal statistical agency in the late 1980s seem not to have been reproduced during the first few years of the post-Soviet period. Thus, nothing comparable to the kind of material shown above in Tables 4.2 and 4.3 has been

Table 4.5

Average Earnings in Sectors of Predominantly Male and Predominantly Female Employment in Percentage of Average Earnings in Russian Economy, Selected Dates, December 1991–August 1994

Sectors of economy	Dec. 1991	Dec. 1992	Sept. 1993	March 1994	Aug. 1994
"Male branches"					
Gas	209	465	297	361	361
Coal	187	243	198	216	206
Oil extraction	241	331	275	240	255
Electric power	201	221	188	236	190
"Female branches"					
Textiles	122	81	71	62	49
Food	127	135	129	124	127
Instrument making	77	58	83	58	55
Trade and public catering	78	73	81	81	83
Health care	69	60	78	80	80
Education	64	70	71	77	62
Culture and art	60	48	57	66	56

Source: Ekonomicheskie novosti Rossii i Sodruzhestvo, 1995, no. 1 (January).

Note: Our source makes it clear that these calculations are drawn from Goskomstat data.

released for the period 1992–95. One thing is certain, however. In the first year of stepped-up market reform, average earnings in sectors of predominantly female employment like public education and health care—already well below the national average—fell even further behind average earnings in the economy as a whole. Thus, earnings in the health care sector in 1992 (where women comprised 83 percent of those employed) were 63.6 percent of the national average wage, down from 75.4 percent during the previous year. In public education (with female employment at about 79 percent of the total) average earnings in 1992 fell to 60 percent of earnings in the economy as a whole, compared to 70.4 percent in 1991.[25] If we take a broader range of "women's branches" (see Table 4.5), it appears that by 1993–94 some of these sectors had recovered or even slightly exceeded the (comparatively low) relative earnings level they had attained on the eve of the reforms (in December 1991). However, by 1994 the relative position of most of the "women's branches" shown in Table 4.6 had either declined since the end of 1991 or remained essentially stable.

Table 4.6

Ratio of Average Salaries of Health Care and Public Education Employees to Wage-Earners in Male-Dominated Industries in October 1994

	Males as a percentage of total employment	Ratio of salaries in health care and education to wages in male-dominated industries
Oil extraction	70.2	0.20
Oil refining	57.7	0.27
Natural gas	64.7	0.31
Coal extraction	97.2	0.27
Ferrous metallurgy	65.4	0.57
Petrochemical	52.5	0.76
Air transport	65.0	0.22
Machine tool	58.0	0.81
Metal fabrication	70.0	0.93
Dairy industry	84.3	0.52
Construction	75.0	0.31
Drilling	84.0	0.19

Source: State Committee of the Russian Federation on Statistics (Goskomstat), *Itogi vyborochnogo obsledovaniia zarabotnoi platy rabotnikov po otdel'nym professiam i dolzhnostiam za oktiabr 1994 goda* (Moscow, 1995), pp. 7–8.

The wage gap is more sharply revealed when the average wages of health care and public education employees are compared with average wages in traditionally male-dominated industries. As Table 4.6 shows, in October 1994, women in the health and education sectors, despite higher educational attainments, earned one-third or less of the wages of the workers in most of the male-dominated branches of the economy. The relative wages in the predominantly female health care and education sectors fell even further in 1995, dropping from 79 and 73 percent, respectively, to 68 and 62 percent of the average wage. The impact of market-oriented reforms was apparently more painful for those employed in these sectors than for job-holders in the predominantly male-dominated fuel and energy sectors. Responding in part to the concerns of workers in the budgetary sectors and to the upcoming elections in December 1995, President Yeltsin issued a decree almost doubling their wages in November 1995. The plight of some losing groups was clearly beginning to play a role in influencing the direction of economic reform.[26]

Table 4.7

Percent Distribution of Female Wages in Different Sectors, April 1994

Wages[a] (in thous. rubles)	Industry and construction	Social sector	Finance	Trade	Transport and communication
Less than 20	6.0	4.6	1.1	1.9	1.9
20–50	25.2	19.9	7.6	18.2	9.3
50–100	41.1	44.1	22.8	37.7	27.8
100–150	18.4	18.5	30.4	23.5	33.3
150–200	7.1	8.6	20.6	9.8	16.7
200–300	1.3	4.0	12.0	4.5	7.3
More than 300	0.9	0.3	5.5	4.4	3.7

Source: Institute of Economics, Center for Labor Studies, *The Position of Women in a Reforming Economy: The Russian Experience* (Moscow, 1995), pp. 33–34.

Note: Table based on a survey of 1,088 women in Ivanovo and Nizhnii Novgorod.

[a]Average wage for 1994 = 171,500 rubles. Minimum subsistence wage for 1994 = 76,660 rubles.

When we look at the distribution of women's wages *within* various branches of the economy we can clearly see that women were employed mainly in low-wage jobs in both low- and high-wage sectors. As Table 4.7 reveals, in April 1994 most women earned less than the average wage of 171,500 rubles in all economic sectors. In industry, construction, trade, and the social sectors, a majority of women received wages close to or below the subsistence minimum of 76,660 rubles.

While wage differentials between men and women within all major industrial sectors were narrower than the average gender wage gap of approximately 70 percent for the economy as a whole, wage differences between men and women within particular industries still reveal an increasing tendency toward gender inequalities. As Table 4.8 shows, gender wage differentials within industries tended to decline between 1991 and 1992, but began to increase once again in 1994. Generally, gender wage differentials have been higher in male-dominated industries than in female-dominated branches of the economy.

Why is the average gender wage gap for the economy as a whole so much higher than gender wage differentials within industries? The answer can be traced to the continuing practice of crowding women into relatively lower wage sectors and occupations. The occupational segregation of women tends to diminish the value of their skills and education. These trends are clearly demonstrated in Table 4.9, which

Table 4.8

Female Wages as a Percentage of Male Wages in Different Industries, 1990–1994

Sector	1990		1991		1992		1993		1994	
	Workers	Employees	Workers	Employees	Workers	Employees	Workers	Employees	Workers	Employees
Metallurgy	82.7	84.2	84.6	85.9	89.5	95.4	82.0	91.5	75.5	85.1
Engineering	84.7	86.5	83.9	86.4	92.2	91.3	85.8	83.5	77.1	82.0
Chemical	93.0	95.4	91.4	93.6	90.7	92.0	92.7	91.3	91.3	86.8
Building materials	86.5	85.3	87.5	87.7	92.4	93.3	82.3	83.7	87.5	91.9
Wood and paper	88.9	90.4	88.6	89.1	91.2	91.7	93.0	92.5	84.4	84.8
Light industry	94.7	93.7	93.5	93.5	94.6	93.9	99.1	95.0	96.5	92.5
Food	91.3	90.6	90.9	90.0	101.7	102.8	99.3	96.5	93.2	92.0
Averages	88.7	89.2	88.1	89.1	94.2	94.2	91.7	89.7	86.7	87.5

Source: Institute of Economics, Center for Labor Studies, *The Position of Women in a Reforming Economy: The Russian Experience* (Moscow, 1995), pp. 33–34.

Table 4.9

Distribution by Gender of Professional and Skill Groupings of Workers and Employees, 1993

Qualification group	Percent distribution		Relative wages of qualification groups as a percentage of unskilled workers' wages
	Male	Female	
Unskilled service worker	30.9	69.1	60
Skilled service worker	21.1	78.9	111
Unskilled worker	61.1	38.9	100
Semi-skilled worker	64.9	35.1	132
Skilled worker	85.9	14.1	152
Semi-skilled office worker	8.5	91.5	86
Semi-skilled specialist	28.0	72.0	104
Skilled specialist	39.4	60.6	140
Low/middle manager	55.3	44.7	156
High-level manager	70.3	29.7	432
People in new market infrastructure	81.9	18.1	340

Source: Institute of Economics, Center for Labor Studies, *The Position of Women in a Reforming Economy: The Russian Experience* (Moscow, 1995), pp. 15, 40.
Note: Source indicates data based on a survey of four Russian cities.

shows the relative wages of different occupational groups and their relationship to gender segmentation. The picture that emerges indicates that the level of skill and education is not a predictor of the relative wages of men and women. More important is the concentration of men and women into particular occupational groups. Thus, skilled professionals—a group that mainly encompassed women—earned less than skilled workers—a male-dominated job classification, and semi-skilled office workers—a female occupation—earned less than unskilled male workers.

Some economists dismiss concerns about women's relatively low wages, arguing that women freely choose low-wage jobs because they view their income as supplementary to their husbands' wages. A majority of women are indeed part of two-income families, but a significant proportion cannot rely on their husbands' salaries. According to one recent survey, as many as 35 percent of all women, married or not, depend on their own income to support themselves and their families.[27]

The evidence of women's deteriorating economic position presented thus far relates to employed women. But other demographic and social factors have contributed to women's vulnerable position after the collapse of communism. Women live longer than men and outnumber men two to one in the population over age sixty. Since they can also retire earlier, women accounted for approximately 72 percent of all retirees in 1992.[28] After the fall of communism, the real value of pensions declined even more sharply than average wages. In 1991, the average pension was 49 percent of the average wage; it dropped to 35 percent in 1996. For most of 1995, the average pension was below the subsistence minimum level for pensioners. Clearly, women fared worse than the average pensioner. The bleak economic outlook of many of the mostly women pensioners accounts for their increasing support of the reformed Communist Party and their rejection of Yeltsin's economic policies. While Yeltsin ordered a 50 percent increase in supplementary pension payments to pensioners in January 1996 (which helped raise the average pension above the subsistence minimum for retirees), it is doubtful that this measure will significantly change the strong anti-reformist sentiments of this group of elderly (mainly women) Russians.

Female-headed households are especially vulnerable to declining child allowances and services. Declining child–care services undermine women's ability to participate in paid employment. In 1990 there were 9 million children in nurseries and kindergartens; by 1995 there were less than 6 million. In the late 1980s 8 million schoolchildren participated in summer camps; in the mid-1990s the number dropped by approximately 50 percent.[29]

Child allowances have fallen dramatically. Subsidies for children are pegged to the minimum wage rather than to estimates of the minimum amount necessary to care for children. Since the minimum wage was approximately 20 percent of the average wage in 1995, and has lagged behind increases in the average wage,[30] child allowances provided little protection against the rising costs of child care. The failure to address this issue is one of the factors influencing the feminization of poverty.

Declining Employment Opportunities

While the early stages of marketization at the very least reproduced, and in all probability reinforced, the preexisting earning gap between men and women, and pushed more women into poverty, the emerging market economy also ended the Soviet goal of fully integrating women into the labor force. If the "forced emancipation" of women did not end gender inequality, the emerging market economy added a new concern—job insecurity. With marketization, Russia has moved from a full employment economy to one characterized by growing labor surpluses. Declining employment opportunities have affected women differently than men.

Faced with increasing job competition, women have been more likely than men to withdraw from paid employment. During the period 1992 to 1995, total employment declined by 4.1 million.[31] Approximately one-half of the decline (2.1 million) can be attributed to growing unemployment; the other half to decreasing labor force participation.

Early concerns that unemployment would have a woman's face have not materialized. Men accounted for approximately 55.3 percent of the 7.8 percent of the unemployed in March 1995. Total unemployment is much higher if one includes those forced to take unpaid administrative leaves or to work part-time. Some female branches of the economy have been especially affected by these problems. But hidden unemployment does not seem to be particularly a women's issue and is therefore discussed more fully in the next chapter.

However, women do constitute the overwhelming proportion of the population who have dropped out of the labor force. Their share of the total labor force, already declining in the last few years of Soviet rule, fell from 52 percent in 1991 to 47 percent in 1995. Since 1991, women have been ten times more likely than men to leave the labor force. They have chosen either to retire or to stay at home. The few who have chosen full-time housework come from families with relatively high per capita incomes in which the husbands are part of the new entrepreneurial class or business elite. For the less fortunate, the decision to leave the labor force was not freely chosen. The decline in women's labor force participation has taken place at a time when real income—both household and individual—was substantially below the pre-reform levels. It seems likely, therefore, that for most women the decision to leave or not to seek paid employment is a reflection of declining economic opportunities and available child–care services rather than a freely chosen desire for more family or leisure time.

The New Debate on Gender Inequality

Feminist critics continued to be heard during 1992–95. But now they contended that a new problem had appeared: "open, direct sexual discrimination" had increasingly come to replace the "hidden indirect discrimination common under Soviet socialism." Feminists claimed that such discrimination was now common in the hiring, promotion, retraining, and firing of personnel. Most women agreed. In a survey taken in 1994, a majority of women claimed that they did not have the same opportunities as men in hiring and job advancement.[32] Hence, the urgent need for policies that would promote a "gender-neutral" social and economic structure, policies that would presumably embody the principle of equality of opportunity.[33]

But a rather pessimistic outlook that had not appeared in feminist discourse during the years of perestroika was now evident. Some feminists acknowledged that the ideology and practice of social equality had been so discredited during the period of state socialism that an egalitarian social policy stood little chance of being successfully implemented. By implication, the best that could be hoped for during the market transition was some limit on the growth of gender inequality rather than its reduction. Such a reduction could hardly be expected in an environment which some feminists characterized as "a postsocialist patriarchal renaissance."

Some economists associated with the Institute of Economics strongly disagreed with the rising feminist alarm about increasing gender discrimination. They argued that gender differences in employment reflected market choices and outcomes rather than gender discrimination. If Soviet ideology proclaimed the virtues of equality and obscured the reality of gender discrimination and inequality, market ideologists now viewed gender differences more positively, arguing that gender inequalities were a natural consequence of market forces.

Looking through the lens of the marketplace, these critics of feminism associated women's declining labor force participation with the characteristics women brought to the job market—characteristics that they claimed undermined women's competitiveness. These included the costs of "social protection" (maternity leave, breaks during working hours, time off to care for children), women's lag in vocational training and work skills, and the expectation that women were simply psychologically unprepared to function effectively in a competitive job market; all these elements pointed to reduced female employment as a normal accompaniment to the market transition.[34] Those who stressed the normalcy and desirability of a reduced role for women in the workforce in the course of the market transition left little doubt about their positive assessment of the benefits the market would ultimately bring: "Three generations of Soviet people became accustomed to expecting the state to decide many of the problems that, under conditions of a market and competition, each individual decides for himself and regards this not only as his obligation but also as a privilege, since such a position makes him feel that he is not an object of the social policy of the state but an active subject of the changes taking place in society."[35]

The sharpest criticism of the feminist perspective has come from social scientists associated with the Institute of Economics, Center for Labor Market Studies. In a recent publication they argued that:

> The existence of problems of socio-economic differences in the situation of men and women, has been confirmed and developed since the beginning of the century by feminism, which has directed its efforts at equalizing the starting conditions of social and economic activity of men and women. However, concentrating their attention on aspects of social equality and the protection of the rights of women, feminists have ignored the objective roots generating "inequality" and reproducing it. They have reduced the problem to the subjective aggressiveness and social domination of men.[36]

These critics of feminism recognize that there is still a strict division of professions into "male" and "female" and that "female jobs are mostly not well paid."[37] But they ask why those divisions should be seen as a symptom of gender discrimination rather than as a consequence of the free choices men and women make. Would such choices, they ask, be considered discriminatory if women had chosen "typical 'male' professions such as taxi driver, crane operator etc."?[38] They claim that there is no justification for assuming that sexual differentiation in the labor market is caused by discrimination since "the conditions of recruitment, advancement within a company, and social benefits are almost the same for men and women."[39]

What, then, are the "objective roots" of men's and women's labor market choices? Women, according to the new market ideologists, are more likely to choose low-wage jobs and occupations because "in an average family their wages are mostly supplementary." Since women are less dependent on their own income, unlike men they are also more likely to accept wages that are low relative to their skill level. The critics of feminism recognize that a wage structure that undervalues a worker's qualifications might reduce work effort and motivation and therefore, "might give employers the wrong impression about the lower quality of female labor in comparison to that of men." Without examining the broader implications of such wage disparities on worker efficiency, they suggest instead that "working less intensively is suitable for women . . . because their main task is housekeeping." They conclude that "the interest of working women will be best protected by increasing labor market flexibility, developing new forms of employment and making it possible to consider the needs of women in both the labor market and household spheres as well as developing the service sector."[40]

In accepting the gendered construction of the labor market, the new market ideologists fail to consider the ways in which the market reinforces gender stereotypes that undermine the position of women in the economy and society. It is remarkable that after so many years of full-time labor force participation, and their relatively high educational and professional attainments, women are still viewed as secondary workers. The Russian experience clearly demonstrates that the full participation of women in the labor force by itself does not eliminate gender stereotypes. To address problems of gender discrimination and inequality, social policy must ultimately confront the deeper cultural and ideological roots of gender differences.*

The assumption that women bear the primary responsibility for the household continues to limit women's labor market choices and promotes labor market segmentation and inequality, exacerbating women's economic and social problems during the market transition. But more open gender discrimination also reinforces gender divisions. One recent report revealed that it has become common practice to specify gender in announcements of available job vacancies.[41] Faced with more limited opportunities in job placements and professional advancement, women are losing ground in their search for greater freedom of choice.

Women are not alone in bearing the costs of gender inequality. It

---

*The cultural aspect of gender inequality was clearly revealed at a conference on problems of the market transition in Russia organized by the authors. After one of the founders of feminism in Russia presented her arguments about post-Soviet gender inequality, a leading Russian expert on social stratification approached her and asked,"Why should a woman as beautiful and talented as you waste your time on such a trivial issue?"

also imposes significant social costs on the economy and society. A declining birthrate and increasing incidence of infant mortality are a reflection in part of women's declining reproductive health and economic position. Furthermore, the mismatch between a woman's relatively low wages and her high educational qualifications reduces both the return on investments in education and productivity. Market efficiency considerations suggest that there could be considerable economic gains if the gendered construction of the labor market were modified.

Despite the strong feminist criticism of the impact of radical market reforms on women, feminists display no particular nostalgia for the situation that prevailed in the Soviet era. Most references to the status of women during that period are critical. Still, criticism has become tempered by expressions of concern that some of the past opportunities available to women are threatened by the kind of market transition in progress. For example, one publication of the Institute of Socioeconomic Problems of the Population (an organization that created the Center for Gender Studies and from which some of the initial feminist literature emerged), appealed for a return to the "positive" features of the past and noted the following: "As many studies show, women think that at the preceding stage of the country's development they had greater opportunities for normal professional growth. . . . For example, the need to restore the previous role of kindergartens is quite obvious. Their absence today is much more tragic than the deficiencies in their work that are familiar to everybody."[42]

Similar concerns were expressed—albeit in passing—in the course of a review of Western feminist writings that appeared in 1994 in the principal Russian philosophy journal. The author, N.S. Iulina, noted that there was a "real danger of losing everything positive that we attained in the Soviet period." Of course, the emancipatory slogans of that period often functioned as a cover for a policy of "intensive exploitation of women's labor." But the rhetoric of "equality of the sexes" also had healthy consequences. It "dictated rules of the game and behavior according to which it was indecent to treat a woman as a 'secondary' object whose reason for existence was to serve the needs of the family and the man." Iulina was particularly concerned that the development of a market system under Russian conditions, unless accompanied by the kinds of "counter-weights of a social, legal and moral nature worked out in economically developed countries," would reinforce the influences of "patriarchal" approaches to the proper role of women in the family and society.[43]

But an occasional favorable reference to some aspect of the Soviet heritage does not reflect a yearning for the reimposition of Soviet rule. Nor do these views imply a rejection of the general idea of transition to a market economy, as long as the emerging market system is seen as compatible with the existence of such institutions as free or low-cost child-care facilities that prevailed in the Soviet period and generally exist in many economically advanced societies. But these views do reflect the genuine fears and concerns of a substantial group of "losers" or, more precisely, those who speak for them. Moreover, these "losers" are not simply women who are primarily oriented to a work career and confront steadily decreasing employment opportunities and a rising male–female earnings gap. They also include pensioners and women oriented primarily to child-rearing and "housekeeping" roles whose newly enforced "emancipation" from their traditional work duties is occurring at a time when their real incomes have fallen below pre-reform levels.

5

Wage-Earners: Winners and Losers

Prior to the collapse of communism, democratically oriented reformers looked to the market as a means of transforming the Soviet culture of work. In their view, decades of state socialism had created a state-dependent worker reluctant to take risks, to display initiative, to assume responsibility, to make independent decisions—that is, to exhibit a market mentality. According to Tat´iana Zaslavskaia, the market would alter this "state-dependent mentality" by creating incentives that rewarded those managers and workers who "work better, run their operations more intelligently and prudently," and "are more aware of technological progress."[1] As a result of such changes, the living conditions of most Russians would improve.

Reformers were aware that the transition to the market would entail some social costs. According to Leonid Gordon, an adviser to the newly formed independent miner's union, a temporary decline in workers' living standards was an inevitable part of the transition process, "a prerequisite" for the economic expansion that would soon follow. But better living conditions would be ensured if the transition to a "civilized" market could proceed in an environment in which recently independent trade unions were free to represent the interests of workers. Under such conditions, the market would end the long-standing Soviet practice of treating workers' consumption as the residual share of national output available after higher ranking priorities for capital investment and military outlays had been met.[2]

Reformers also understood that marketization would end Soviet-style full employment. While there were substantial differences in estimates of its probable magnitude, it seemed clear that reductions in state subsidies, the elimination of state-fixed production targets, and the privatization of state property would make unemployment unavoidable. While public opinion surveys documented an increasing fear among workers that marketization threatened their jobs, for some reformers such anxiety performed the positive function of heightening people's sense of "personal responsibility for their own fate."[3]

Some reformers cautioned that the market would also increase inequality, "enriching some and ruining others," and not always, as Zaslavskaia warned, "in accordance with efficient economic performance." But most reformers believed that the market was the most reliable instrument for assessing the relative contributions to output of the various participants in the production process and, therefore, for ensuring a more just distribution of income. According to Iurii Volkov, a sociologist associated with an educational institution that served members and functionaries of the official Soviet trade unions, breaking the link between people's income (which in a market system would depend on their contribution to output) and their "official status" (party-state position and "connections") was a necessary step toward greater social justice.[4]

Like other defenders of the market transition, Volkov never claimed that a market economy would eliminate all manifestations of social injustice or denied that its benefits would emerge only in the "long run." But the expectations fostered by such advocates of reform in 1990–92 certainly encouraged the view that the advantages of the market (both in terms of increased living standards and a more "just" distribution of income) would not be very long in coming. It would be difficult to find evidence (at least in the writings we have reviewed above) of expectations that a prolonged period of sacrifice would be necessary.

How quickly their views changed after 1992. Some of the sharpest criticism of the consequences of market reforms were offered by precisely those commentators who had been among the principal advocates of such reforms earlier in the decade (for example, Zaslavskaia and Gordon). Thus, the critiques that follow are not typically an appeal for a return to the state socialist system (indeed, Zaslavskaia characterizes such an attempt as the "path to catastrophe"),[5] but are rather implicit admissions of the oversimplified and overoptimistic view of the market transition that some of its advocates had, and a partial listing of some of the unanticipated problems generated during the early stages of market reforms. Criticism functioned essentially as an appeal to "correct" or "regulate" the market reform process, not to abandon it.

In an article published in 1995, in which she made clear her support for continuing the market reform process, Zaslavskaia confronted adherents of reform with some highly negative assessments of the consequences of the economic transformations implemented thus far. For example, it seemed clear to Zaslavskaia that "the social cost of the transformations was too heavy. It is no accident that most of the population is disappointed in their results."[6] The context of Zaslavskaia's discussion indicates that the substantial decline in the real income of the bulk of wage-earners between the last years of Soviet rule and 1994–95 was the critical factor in her characterization of the market reforms' social cost as excessive. No less important, she also noted that the newly emerging labor market was generating "unprecedentedly sharp and unjustified gaps in the pay of various categories of working people." It was not so much the increase in income differentials that seemed disturbing to Zaslavskaia as the socio-occupational structure of relative incomes. "For example, the work of middlemen, merchants and dealers (not to mention activists in shadowy and criminal economic activity) is paid at much higher rates than the work of producers of necessary and useful output." But this was merely one illustration of the kind of prevailing patterns of income distribution that helped explain why—according to Zaslavskaia's findings—"three quarters of Russians regard the current system of payment of labor as being even less just than the previous system."[7]

The significance of Zaslavskaia's observation can only be appreciated if we recall that some of the early adherents of market reforms seemed to have no doubt that the market transition would involve a movement toward greater "social justice" in the distribution of income. Nor is there anything to suggest that Leonid Gordon anticipated in his early celebration of the market economy the disturbing situation he would find prevailing some three years after the initiation of post-Soviet market reforms. As he noted with concern, "it should be emphasized that the increase in relative and absolute poverty has affected the most skilled part of working people constituting the core of the middle class in developed countries."[8]

Thus, neither Zaslavskaia's identification of some of the principal "winners" in the emerging market economy nor Gordon's identification of some of its principal "losers" suggests a significant movement toward a more just or efficient economy. These assessments were not offered as a repudiation of the transition to a market system. But they did represent implicit admissions that the early views of the emerging market system held by some of its chief proponents were—at least in some respects—idealized and simplistic visions that failed to anticipate the extent of the inequities associated with the market transition.

Zaslavskaia and Gordon were by no means alone in their critical assessments of the impact of market reforms on wage structure and income distribution in 1994–95. No issue evoked more critical comment than this one. Questions were raised about the rationality of the emerging wage structure and its ethical foundations. In one of the more extreme formulations, the sociologist Z.T. Golenkova noted in a 1995 publication: "In Russian society today the violation of the principle of the just payment of labor has become the norm."[9] In Golenkova's view, post-Soviet Russian society had become pervaded by "unjustified social differentiation and polarization" rooted in large income differences that were in no sense based on differences in "the results of labor" and economic performance. In another formulation, Marina Mozhina, a principal researcher at the Institute of Socioeconomic Problems of the Population, warned that the ongoing reforms were creating "complete chaos in the distribution of incomes and the unprecedented growth in the differentiation of wages of different groups of working people, and on this basis the creation of a world of difference between poverty and wealth."[10]

An additional example of the concerns of critics of the newly emerging wage structure should suffice to illustrate the striking differences between the market expectations of 1990–92 and the perception of market realities in 1994–95. In the view of Ekaterina Khibovskaia, a researcher at the Russian Center for Public Opinion Research (whose empirical findings will be examined below), the "excessive state regulation" of the payment of labor that characterized the previous system had been replaced by "an almost complete lack of control." In the absence of adequate state control over the distribution of earnings, the structure of earnings was often, quite simply, "disproportional,"—that is, differences in wage incomes of workers in different socio-occupational groups, industrial branches and sectors of the economy "could not be considered economically grounded and correspondingly justi-

Table 5.1

Average Russian Real Wage Index (1985 = 100)

1985	100
1986	101
1987	104
1988	113
1989	121
1990	132
1991	123
1992	73
1993	83
1994	76
1995	55

Source: Government of the Russian Federation, Russian Economic Trends, vol. 5 (1996), no. 1, pp. 51–52.

fied." Khibovskaia then concluded her analysis by explicitly denying the adequacy of exclusive reliance on the market mechanism. "We can hardly assume that the market mechanism will eliminate the disproportions without the intervention of the state, the strengthening of which should be directed toward the search for regulatory influences of an economic, and not a prohibitive character."[11] Clearly, the celebration of the market encouraged by some of the promarket literature of the early 1990s began to be replaced by a more balanced approach as the impact of the market on the Russian post-Soviet environment made itself felt.

Changing Structure of Wages and Wage Levels

What evidence did these critics draw on to support their increasing alarm about declining real wages and what they perceived as an unjustified pattern of wage inequality? In Chapter 2 we briefly reviewed some of the general trends in wages. Table 5.1 provides a more complete picture of official estimates of declining average real wages for the period 1985–95.

Given the widespread public association of declining living standards with the final years of the Soviet regime, it is worth noting that Table 5.1 shows a steady increase in average real wages over the period 1985–90. Indeed, by 1990 average real wages were almost one-third greater than their 1985 level. It is somewhat ironic that the period

Table 5.2

Distribution of Aggregate Wage Bill by Quintiles (%)

	Sept. 1991	Sept.1994
Total	100.0	100.0
First quintile	7.7	3.9
Second quintile	12.6	8.4
Third quintile	16.9	13.9
Fourth quintile	22.9	22.4
Fifth quintile	39.9	51.4

Source: OECD, *Wage Formation During the Period of Economic Restructuring in the Russian Federation* (Paris, 1995), p. 37.

1991–92, which witnessed a sharp decline in real wages, was also the period in which the proponents of the market transition suggested that it was only a matter of time before the functioning of the market mechanism would enhance both social justice and economic performance. As Table 5.1 suggests, by the end of 1995 that time had not yet arrived. Average real wages in 1995 had fallen to 45 percent of their 1991 level.

The sharp decline in real wages exhibited at the beginning of 1992 reflects the explosion of prices after liberalization, a process unaccompanied by anything approaching a comparable enhancement of wage rates. Thereafter, real wages continued to fall in tandem with inflation and sharply declining output and productivity. Of course, as we noted in chapter 2, for a minority of wage-earners the decline in real wages was partially compensated by the opening up of opportunities for alternative sources of income associated with privatization. However, most observers accept Leonid Gordon's assessment that "a general decline in real aggregate incomes for the bulk of the population cannot be doubted."[12]

Aside from the substantial decline in average real wages during the first half of the 1990s, there is also evidence of considerable increases in wage inequality. Table 5.2 reveals that in just three years (September 1991 to September 1994) the redistribution of wage incomes from the lowest to the highest income groups was no minor matter. Thus the share of income received by the top fifth of wage recipients increased from less than 40 percent of the aggregate wage bill to more than half, while the share of the lowest quintile fell from 7.7 percent of the wage bill to less than 4 percent. Increasing inequality, coming in the midst of a period of declining average real wages and reduced output, could hardly be expected to contribute to the enhanced sense of social justice anticipated by some of the early over-optimistic predictions about the market transition. However, as noted earlier, the widespread sense of grievance generated by changes in the distribution of wage income was not directed primarily at the general principle of increased inequality as such, but mainly at the specific pattern of "winners" and "losers" that accompanied increased distributional inequality.

What were some of the specific changes in wage structure associated with the reforms of the early 1990s that help explain the marked increase in wage inequality shown in Table 5.2? One fairly obvious factor at work here was the policy of raising wages in most of the relatively low-paid budgetary sectors (education, health care, culture, and art) at a much slower rate than in the nonbudgetary sectors, particularly in the relatively high-wage extractive industries. The sharply contrasting rates of growth of wages between 1989 and 1992 of miners on the one hand, and schoolteachers, college professors, and physicians on the other hand (see Table 5.3), can be regarded as a harbinger of a more general trend. While money wages of educators and physicians increased in the range of five to fourteen times, coal miners' earnings exhibited a twenty-five-fold rise during this period.*

A more comprehensive picture of the wage structure that reveals sharply increasing wage inequality in the early post-Soviet period is provided in Table 5.4. The principal "winners" (groups whose earnings increased more rapidly than average earnings in the economy as a whole) included—along with coal miners—wage-earners employed in the oil extraction, oil refining, and gas industries, groups whose earnings were well above the economywide average even in the pre-reform period.

Average wages in the financial sectors (banking and insurance) also grew rapidly during this period. Financial institutions were restructured, and new ones proliferated as part of the process of marketization and the transfer of Russia's immense wealth into private hands. Investments in financial assets rather than new capital equipment stimulated

---

*The coal miners' relative wage advantage should not be interpreted as an indicator of their increased well-being. Delayed wage payments, short-time work, deteriorating working conditions, declining employment opportunities, and inflation have undermined their standard of living.

Table 5.3

**Estimated Average Monthly Earnings of Miners and Selected
Budgetary-Sector Occupations in Russia, 1989 and May 1992**
(rubles per month)

	Average monthly earnings	
Occupational group	1989	May 1992
Miners	600	15,000
Physicians	160	2,250[a]
Teachers	175	2,300[a]
College professors	550	3,000[a]

Source: B. Raizberg, "How Much We Are Paid, How Much We Can Be and Should Be Paid," *Ekonomika i zhizn'*, May 1992, no. 22, p. 1.

[a]The source specifies that these figures are based on data of the State Committee on Statistics (Goskomstat) of the Russian Federation, with due regard for "decisions taken to increase wages in May 1992."

demand for employment in this sector. The lure of higher wages attracted many younger, educated individuals into these new financial and business services. The relatively privileged position of these employees is also reflected in the much higher relative level of fringe benefits they received. In 1994, the value of fringe benefits in the financial sector amounted to 32 percent of average monthly wages compared to only 10 percent for the economy as a whole.[13]

Losing groups included not only most of the relatively low-paid budgetary sector employees[14] (teachers as well as those in the "culture and art" and science divisions of the budgetary sector), but also wage-earners in light industry, agriculture, and the machine-building and metal-working sectors. What is clear, in any case, is that the interindustry wage differentials prevailing in the final years of the Soviet era tended to be reinforced in the early post-Soviet period.

We do not offer anything approximating a comprehensive explanation of why this occurred. But one key factor has been the continuing pattern of monopolization in certain product markets. Thus, wages in the monopolistically organized transportation sector rose from 20 to 50 percent above the average wage level. The significantly higher increases in wages in the fuel sector also reflected this branch's greater economic power in the product market.

Market power in the energy industry was reinforced by the continu-

Table 5.4

Average Monthly Wages, by Sector, in Russian Economy, 1991, 1993, 1994

Sectors	1991		1993		1994	
	In rubles	In percentage of average for economy as a whole	In thous. rubles	In percentage of average for economy as a whole	In thous. rubles	In percentage of average for economy as a whole
Economy as a whole	548	100	58.7	100	220.3	100
Industry	606	111	63.4	108	228.5	104
Electric power	917	167	122.9	210	451.0	205
Fuel	1,001	183	149.5	255	521.2	237
Oil extracting	1,107	202	182.6	311	576.6	262
Oil refining	663	121	119.9	204	456.8	207
Gas	1,129	206	235.8	402	987.2	448
Coal	1,085	198	146.4	250	507.1	230
Ferrous metallurgy	696	127	83.9	143	266.6	121
Nonferrous metallurgy	967	177	126.9	216	434.0	197
Chemical and petrochemical	590	108	59.4	101	207.1	94
Machine building and metal working	529	96	48.4	83	175.9	80
Timber, woodworking, pulp, and paper	587	107	52.6	90	183.6	83
Building materials	649	118	67.7	115	250.3	114

(continued)

Table 5.4 (continued)

Glass and porcelain	564	103	48.3	82	n.a.	
Light	575	105	41.4	71	118.0	54
Food	653	119	76.4	130	268.8	122
Printing	527	96	53.2	91	n.a.	
Agriculture	459	84	36.0	61	111.3	51
Construction	695	127	78.0	133	283.3	129
Transport	655	120	88.4	151	330.2	150
Health care, physical culture, and social security	416	76	44.6	76	167.8	76
Education	389	71	40.1	68	152.2	69
Culture and art	369	67	36.4	62	137.0	62
Science and science services	515	94	39.6	68	171.7	78
Banking and insurance	986	180	142.6	243	459.4	209

Sources: Data for 1991 and 1993 are from Z. Ryzhikova, "Wages in Branches of the National Economy," *Ekonomist*, 1994, no. 12, p. 22; the material for 1994 is from Goskomstat, *Informatsionnyi statisticheskii biulleten'*, 1995, no. 13 (November), pp. 21–22. The figures showing the percentage relationship between monthly earnings in the individual sectors and average earnings in the economy as a whole in 1994 are based on our calculations. For 1991 and 1993 these figures are in the first source cited above.

ing symbiotic connections between political and economic power. Although traditional Soviet-style centralized control over wage differentials by industry and sector clearly weakened during the period under consideration, the highly unequal lobbying power of the executives of different industries also helps explain why wage levels in some sectors increased much more than in others. Thus, it would not be unreasonable to suppose that the relatively favorable treatment of wage-earners in the fuel branches (particularly in the gas industry) had some connection with the fact that Prime Minister Chernomyrdin had formerly been the chief executive of the Soviet gas monopoly. Similarly, it would not be far-fetched to suggest that the relatively generous treatment of coal miners was influenced by President Yeltsin's need to retain the political allegiance of a group of militant workers who had the potential of shutting down their industry.

As we noted earlier, another important factor influencing the pattern of wage inequality has been the depressing effect of government budget constraints on the wages of people working in the budgetary sectors and in the still relatively large military-related branches of the economy. While the government could not contain wage increases in industries with significant market power, restrictions in the budget and military-connected sectors resulted in deteriorating wages of what some call the "mass intelligentsia": engineers, scientists, technicians, and skilled workers employed in the machine-building and metal-working industries and doctors, artists, teachers, researchers, and other specialists of comparable skills paid through the state budget. The declining income of many engineers, scientists, technicians, and skilled workers also reflected the substantial decline in spending on capital goods that has characterized the post-Soviet period. As a consequence of these trends, Russia's highly respected research base constructed during the Soviet era is rapidly deteriorating and will not be so easily replaced.[15]

The plight of Russia's "mass intelligentsia" was examined by Tat'iana Zaslavskaia. Writing in 1995, and summarizing her findings concerning the economic status of the country's principal socio-occupational groups, Zaslavskaia noted that "the level of material well-being" of the mass intelligentsia was "quite low," and that the poverty rate among this group was essentially the same as that among the mass of industrial workers—somewhat over 40 percent.[16] (Poverty rates are derived by Zaslavskaia by comparing respondents' estimates of the "subsistence minimum" with their actual earnings.) The failure of the mass intelligentsia to experience any significant improvement in its relative economic status by the mid-1990s seems all the more significant in light of the following. Approximately three-fourths of this social group had some higher education (among industrial workers, three-fourths had an incomplete or complete secondary education). Moreover, during the perestroika period the intelligentsia, by and large, had been a principal supporter of the reform process. But now, in the mid-1990s, Zaslavskaia noted that "the reforms of the recent period have, above all, struck a blow precisely against the intelligentsia." It would be simplistic, of course, to attribute the perpetuation of the relatively low economic status of the intelligentsia (and, in particular, the similarity of its poverty rate to that of industrial workers) to a single factor. But it would also be naive to ignore the implications of the following: 70 percent of the mass intelligentsia category identified by Zaslavskaia were women; 70 percent of Zaslavskaia's industrial workers' stratum were men.

Certain distinctive changes in the structure of relative wages within industries have also contributed to the growth of wage inequality. Interestingly, there has been no persuasive evidence of increased wage differentials among workers based on skill. Indeed, an OECD study found that among worker occupations, "wage differentials according to skills have narrowed compared to the pre-reform period."[17] Nor is it possible to demonstrate that the wage gap between workers and the bulk of engineering-technical personnel increased in the early post-Soviet years.[18]

Who, then, have been the principal winners in the changing distribution of wages and salaries? Direct comparisons of the occupational wage structure in the late Soviet and early post-Soviet periods are not available, but both Russian and Western studies support the view that the largest earnings increases (in both absolute and relative terms) were concentrated in the upper extreme of the wage structure. More specifically, this means that the principal winners have been enterprise directors, top managers, and (in some cases) "chief specialists." Management groups rather than workers, therefore, have been the real winners as a result of the increased economic independence granted to both private and state enterprises. As a study by the Institute of Socioeconomic Problems of the Population put it, "since the level of inflation makes investment in production senseless," the funds and

Table 5.5

Wage Differentials by Socio-Occupational Groups, June 1994

Socio-occupational groups	Average monthly wage of the group in percentage of the average monthly wage of skilled urban workers
Top managers, chief specialists	499
Middle managers	151
Specialists	96
Office employees	94
Skilled urban workers	100
Skilled rural workers	70
Unskilled urban workers	64
Unskilled rural workers	52

Source: Ekaterina Khibovskaia, "The Dynamic of Incomes," *Ekonomicheskie i sotsial'nye peremeny: Monitoring obshchestvennogo mneniia*, 1994, no. 6, p. 34.

resources available to top managerial personnel (including state loans at preferential interest rates) "are distributed among the top-level people at enterprises in the form of individual incomes."[19]

A report by the Ministry of Labor of the Russian Federation covering the first half of 1994 cites an earnings gap on the order of twelve to fifteen times between enterprise directors and the "basic mass" of workers, and indicates that this represents an increase in the former wage differentials between these groups.[20] A VTsIOM study (see Table 5.5) applicable to June 1994 suggests a substantially lower wage differential between top managers and chief specialists on the one hand, and urban workers on the other (on the order of five to seven times), but also treats this differential as representing an increase in the traditional earnings gap between these groups.[21]

The emergence of new legal forms of enterprise ownership along with the continued existence of traditional state-owned firms is another important influence on widening wage differentials. The newly emerging types of business organizations were apparently willing and able to pay higher wage rates than state enterprises. The results of a VTsIOM study of wage differentials by type of ownership at various times in 1994 are shown in Table 5.6. According to this study, by mid-1994 wages paid by private companies (including privately leased enterprises that may have still formally belonged to the state) were more than double the average wage at state-owned firms. Wage levels at

Table 5.6

Wage Differentials by Form of Enterprise Ownership, 1994

Type of enterprise	Average wage by type of enterprise in percentage of average wage at state-owned enterprises		
	February	April	June
State-owned enterprises	100	100	100
State joint-stock companies	97	110	106
Collective farms[a]	60	48	58
Leased enterprises	103	207	229
Nonstate joint-stock companies	134	135	142
Private enterprises	218	185	229

Source: Ekaterina Khibovskaia, "The Dynamic of Incomes," *Ekonomicheskie i sotsial'nye peremeny: Monitoring obshchestvennogo mneniia*, 1994, no. 6, p. 35.

[a]It is not clear whether these figures are based exclusively on money payments to farmers or also include payments in kind and the value of goods consumed by farmers directly out of their own output.

nonstate joint-stock companies were in between these two groups, while—not surprisingly—the equivalent of wage payments at collective farms were by far the lowest among all types of enterprises shown in Table 5.6.

Wage determination procedures in state, recently privatized, and newly created private firms differ. In state enterprises and recently privatized firms the government continues to establish basic wage rates, which limits wage flexibility. Freed from such constraints, wages in newly established private firms are determined by profitability and other firm-specific considerations. But part of the difficulty in monitoring wages in newly created private enterprises is that payments are frequently made off the books. In all probability, very high salaries (as high as $200,000 per month in some foreign firms in Moscow) are not included in official statistics.[22]

What remains unclear is whether the relative wage advantage of employment in the private sector (as shown in Table 5.6) was more or less evenly distributed among all occupational groups, or disproportionately concentrated among top management personnel. Precise data to answer this question are unavailable. But evidence of the emergence of a "new rich" whose wealth is concentrated in financial and trade activities suggests top management benefited the most.

Table 5.7

Distribution of Employment by Principal Types of Ownership, 1992–1995
(%)

Ownership sectors	1992	1993	1994	First quarter 1995
State sector	69	53	45	41
Enterprises with mixed ownership[a]	12	18	21	23.2
Private sector	18	28	33	34.3
Total	99	99	99	98.5

Source: Vladimir Gimpelson, "Is Employment in Russia Restructured?" paper presented at the NATO Economic Colloquium, June 26–28, 1996, p. 10.

[a]This applies to joint-stock companies in which the state holds some proportion of the shares.

New Employment Opportunities and Job Insecurity

While there may be some continuities in the Russian wage structure between the Soviet and early post-Soviet years, the economic environment in which the Russian workforce has functioned since 1992 is—at least in some important respects—strikingly different than the situation prevailing in the Soviet era. On the one hand, the privatization process has created new employment opportunities for a variety of legally recognized entrepreneurial strata as well as for wage-earners in a rapidly expanding private sector. Although Russian sources provide differing estimates of the extent of privatization, we rely here on Goskomstat findings which suggest that the private sector accounted for more than one-third of total employment by early 1995 (see Table 5.7), while the state sector absorbed about two-fifths of the employed population. Most of the remaining workers and employees (23.2 percent) were employed at firms officially designated as "enterprises with mixed ownership" (joint-stock companies with some degree of state-held shares). But the principal trend was clearly toward the expansion of the private sector.

On the other hand, it is also clear that the period since 1992 has been characterized by a decline in total employment and a significant rise in both open and concealed unemployment. Table 5.8 shows the decline in total employment between 1992 and 1995 (about 7 percent)

Table 5.8

Total Employment and Its Distribution by Economic Sector, 1992 and 1995

	1992 (in millions)	1995 (in millions)	Percentage change 1992– 1995	1992 (in percent)	1995 (in percent)
Total employed[a]	72.1	67.1	−6.9	100.0	100.0
Economic sectors:					
Industry	21.3	17.2	−19.2	29.6	25.7
Agriculture	10.3	9.9	−3.9	14.3	14.8
Transport and communications	5.6	4.4	−21.4	7.8	6.6[b]
Construction	7.8	6.5	−6.7	11.0	9.7
Trade and catering	5.6	6.5	16.1	7.9	9.7
Commercial services	2.9	3.3	13.8	4.1	4.9
Health, sport, social security	4.2	4.5	7.1	5.9	6.7
Education, culture, art	7.5	7.6	1.3	10.4	11.3
Science	2.3	1.7	−21.7	3.2	2.5
Credit, finances, and insurance	0.5	0.7	40.0	0.7	1.0
Public administration	1.5	1.7	13.3	2.1	2.5
Other	2.1	2.9	38.1	3.0	3.3

Source: Working Center for Economic Reform, Government of the Russian Federation, *Russian Economic Trends*, vol. 4 (1996), no. 4, p. 93.

[a]The figures for total employed do not add up precisely to the sum of the sectors shown here.

[b]The source on which we rely shows a figure of 7.9 percent here, obviously a computational or typographical error.

and the changing distribution of employment among the various sectors of the economy. The increase in employment in expanding sectors like credit, finance, and insurance (up by 40 percent between 1992 and 1995), trade (up by 16 percent), and commercial services (up by 14 percent) was not enough to offset the decline in employment in the country's principal economic sector—industry (down by almost one-fifth)—as well as in such important sectors as transport and communication and construction.[23] It is also worth noting that the largest percentage decline in employment between 1992 and 1995 occurred in the science sector (21.7 percent), not a good omen insofar as future technological advances are concerned.

Clearly, the processes briefly described above have had both their "winners" and "losers." In the chapter that follows, we focus on a principal group of "winners"—the various strata of entrepreneurs that emerged in the course of the privatization process. In the remainder of the current chapter we examine the emergence of a group of "losers"— the unemployed who, like legally recognized private entrepreneurs, represent a comparatively new phenomenon in Russian society. An issue that will obviously require special attention is the marked discrepancy between the substantial decline in gross domestic product in the early 1990s and the comparatively moderate rise in officially reported unemployment (in both its lower and higher versions).

Before turning to available estimates of the actual unemployment rate, it should be recognized that the results of some public opinion surveys reflect the steadily increasing concern of the Russian population with the problem of unemployment. Thus, a study conducted at the beginning of 1995 asked respondents the following question: "Which of the problems of our society disturbs you most of all?" Fully one-half of the respondents cited the growth of unemployment. Studies conducted earlier by VTsIOM showed that at the end of 1992 some 18 percent of respondents considered unemployment an important problem in Russia; by the end of 1993 the comparable figure had risen to 41 percent.[24] At the very least, these findings testify to the increasing familiarity of the Russian public with the problem of unemployment.[25]

As for the actual dimensions of the unemployment problem, two "official" versions of the (open) unemployment rate may serve as the starting point of our analysis (see Table 5.9). Whatever the limitations of these figures, the novelty of a state agency issuing estimates of the Russian unemployment rate should be recognized: no "official" unemployment statistics were apparently issued or collected in the Soviet Union (or Russia) between the early 1930s and the end of the 1980s.

The lower estimates of the joblessness rate shown in Table 5.9 (which indicate a rise in that rate from less than 1 percent in 1992 to 3.5 percent at the beginning of 1996) reflect the number of the unemployed who registered with the Federal Employment Service. Such registration was (and still is) a necessary condition for receiving unemployment benefits. When the phenomenon of unemployment was officially recognized as having returned to Russia after an absence of almost sixty years, the authorities based their initial estimates of the jobless rate on such registration figures. But it soon became apparent that such estimates could not be taken seriously as realistic approximations of the actual (open) unemployment rate. For a variety of reasons, only a minority of the unemployed bother to register with the Federal

Table 5.9

Russian Unemployment Trends, 1992–1995 (End of Year), 1996 (Third Quarter)

Year	Unemployed (based on registration with Federal Employment Service)		Unemployed (based on ILO definition)	
	(millions)	(% of workforce)	(millions)	(% of workforce)
1992	0.6	0.8	3.6	4.8
1993	0.8	1.2	4.1	5.7
1994	1.6	2.4	5.5	7.5
1995	2.3	3.4	6.4	8.8
1996	2.5	3.6	6.7	9.2

Sources: Vladimir Gimpelson, "Is Employment in Russia Restructured?" paper presented at NATO Economic Colloquium, Brussels, June 1996, p. 9; Working Center for Economic Reform, Government of the Russian Federation, *Russian Economic Trends,* Volume 5, no. 3, 1996, p.128.

Employment Service.[26] Thus Goskomstat has begun to provide more realistic "official" estimates of unemployment that are now based on regular labor force surveys and are guided by the ILO definition of the unemployed (essentially, people of working age who are without jobs but are seeking employment). These considerably higher "official" estimates show the unemployment rate rising from 4.8 percent at the end of 1992 to 9.2 percent in the third quarter of 1996 (see Table 5.9). To complicate matters somewhat, it should also be noted that an unofficial and highly respected research organization like VTsIOM estimated the unemployment rate to be 10 percent at the end of 1995.[27]

Thus, the more reasonable estimates available to us suggest an unemployment rate in the neighborhood of 8–10 percent by the middle of the decade. But this is only part of the story. After all, gross domestic product fell by approximately one-third or more between 1991 and 1995. The 8–10 percent unemployment rate was surely not the labor market's only response to this decline in output. This is the context in which the widely recognized phenomenon of underemployment or concealed unemployment enters the picture. The two principal forms assumed by this phenomenon are (a) the assignment of part-time work to wage-earners interested in full-time employment, and (b) placing workers on unpaid (or partially paid) administrative leave. Both of these methods (along with increasingly frequent delayed wage payments) function to reduce wage costs—and workers' real incomes—without involving mass layoffs. Unfortunately, as is so often the case, Russian sources provide differing estimates of the extent of these practices. We accept as reasonable Vladimir Gimpelson's estimate that some 5–6 percent of the workforce had spells of involuntary part-time work or administrative leave during a typical month in 1995.[28] Such estimates appear to lend support to those Russian scholars who suggest that aggregate unemployment—including both the open and concealed variety—was in the neighborhood of 13 percent in 1995.[29]

While the spells of underemployment described above are often of relatively brief duration, they have apparently been experienced by substantial proportions of the workforce. This is suggested by a VTsIOM study conducted at the end of 1995, which found that 18 percent of working respondents had experienced some period of administrative leave over the past three months.[30] The comparatively frequent reliance on short-time work schedules and unpaid administrative leave help explain the relatively high (but declining) rate of voluntary resignations in a period of steadily rising unemployment.[31] To complicate matters further, it should also be noted that some of the underemployed (in the above forms) as well as the "officially" unemployed may have had part-time supplementary work in the "informal" or unrecorded sector.

Frequent reliance on the mechanisms of concealed unemployment is not the only factor that helps explain the marked discrepancy between the (open) unemployment rate and the sharp reduction in output. Clearly, given the marketization process undertaken in the early post-Soviet period, state authorities had to choose between two policy alternatives: (a) forcing unprofitable enterprises into bankruptcy and risking the social and political consequences of the mass layoffs that would accompany such bankruptcies, or (b) providing the kind of financial support for unprofitable enterprises—especially those employing large numbers of workers—that would permit them to continue operating without mass dismissals. The more serious Russian and Western sources appear to agree that alternative (b) was commonly implemented during the first few years of the post-Soviet regime by the granting of "soft" credits and state subsidies.[32] It seems fairly clear that the choice of alternative (b) was a matter of conscious state policy despite the frequent invocation of the rhetoric of "financial stabilization."

But stricter fiscal and monetary policy after 1994 has imposed increased financial constraints on state budgets and enterprises. As a consequence, another form of concealed unemployment has become more significant, the practice of delayed wage payments. Thus, at the end of 1993 the level of wage arrears in industry, construction, and agriculture was in the neighborhood of 17 percent of the monthly wage bill but then rose sharply throughout most of 1994 and 1995. By the beginning of 1996 wage arrears had reached 83 percent of the monthly wage bill.[33]

Two additional factors that help explain the comparatively modest rise in open unemployment should be noted.[34] To some degree, the reluctance of managers to undertake mass dismissals probably reflected the continuing (but obviously declining) impact of Soviet-era "managerial paternalism" toward workers. This sociocultural tradition was clearly related to the chronic labor shortages that characterized the Soviet period, but the deeply rooted attitudes and semifeudal relations that had their origins in that period could hardly be expected to disappear in the immediate post-Soviet era. In addition, a somewhat more pragmatic consideration on the part of managers was at work here. During the period of early privatization, managers' commitment (formal or informal) to keep the bulk of their workers on the payroll was also motivated—at least in part—by the effort to win their support against the threat of takeovers by outside investors. The significance of this factor, as well as of genuine "paternalism," can hardly be formulated in quantitative terms and the impact of both almost certainly diminished as the post-Soviet reform process continued.

Which groups were most affected by the unemployment that emerged as this reform process unfolded? A curious feature of Russian unemployment statistics is the paucity of official material on the composition of the unemployed, whether by occupation or by economic sector. By relying on official data on the considerable regional differentials in unemployment rates, Russian scholars in this area have sought to identify the sectors and industries that have been most affected by joblessness. On this basis (by identifying the principal economic sectors located in regions with unusually high rates of officially "registered" jobless in 1993–95), the following sectors may be regarded—in the language of Kosmarskii and Maleva—as "leaders in unemployment": the military-industrial complex, machine building and metal working (reflecting the sharp decline in capital investment), light industry, and the timber and woodworking industries.[35] It is surely no accident that there was considerable overlap between the regions (and industries) exhibiting the highest rates of unemployment and those which underwent unusually large declines in the population's real income.[36]

As for the occupational composition of the unemployed, an interesting feature of the scanty Russian material available on this theme is that it focuses largely on gender differentials in the occupational status of the unemployed. Table 5.10 shows the results of Goskomstat studies of the occupational backgrounds of male and female members of the labor force who were jobless at the end of 1993 and 1995. These findings point to rather significant differences in the occupational status of unemployed men and women. Thus, approximately one-third of all jobless women in both years were classified as specialists (29–30 percent) or managerial personnel (3 percent), while the proportion of unemployed men in these occupational categories was less than one-half the comparable figure for women. The specialist's category generally includes fairly skilled personnel with higher than average levels of education. Among the specific occupational groups included here are engineering-technical personnel, teachers, economists, architects, city planners, and medical personnel. The relatively high proportion of female jobless drawn from specialists[37] and managerial staffs helps explain why close to one-quarter of all unemployed in 1993 and 1995—judging by the findings of the Goskomstat studies shown in Table 5.10—fell into these two broad categories. The other side of the picture discussed here is that the proportion of unemployed men drawn from workers' occupations (72–73 percent) was well above the comparable figures for unemployed women (50–53 percent).

Thus far, our main focus has been on the diversity of estimates and manifestations of Russian unemployment, and the scanty data available on the composition of the unemployed by sector and occupation. Nonetheless, the main point that emerges here should not be lost: the Russian unemployment problem has been kept within rather modest dimensions relative to the experience of most East European countries undergoing similar transformation, and relative to the substantial decline in domestic output. Little wonder that ILO estimates suggest a not very modest decline in Russian labor productivity of about 44 percent between 1990 and 1995.[38]

Russia's Great Depression, which began in 1991 and accelerated sharply after the implementation of radical economic reform, did not

Table 5.10

Composition of Unemployed by Occupational Category, End of 1993 and 1995 (% distribution)

Occupational category	Unemployed women, 1993	Unemployed men, 1993	Total unemployed, 1993	Unemployed women, 1995	Unemployed men, 1995	Total unemployed, 1995
Managerial personnel	3.0	2.9	3.0	3.0	2.6	2.8
Specialists	30.3	12.2	21.1	28.7	11.9	19.9
Nonspecialist white-collar employees	4.4	1.0	2.7	4.5	1.4	2.9
Workers	50.3	71.6	61.2	53.4	73.3	63.8
Individuals having no specialty	12.0	12.3	12.0	10.4	10.8	10.6
Total, all categories	100.0	100.0	100.0	100.0	100.0	100.0

Sources: E.G. Gruzdeva, *Zhenskaia bezrabotitsa v Rossii (1991–1994 gg.)* (Moscow, 1995), p. 34; Goskomstat Rossii, *Uroven zhizni naseleniia Rossiiskoe federatsii* (Moscow, 1995), p. 22; Goskomstat Rossii, *Uroven zhizni naseleniia Rossii* (Moscow, 1996), p. 24.

Note: The sources on which we rely indicate that the 1993 figures apply to "the end of 1993" and the 1995 figures apply to "the end of October 1995."

result in massive open joblessness but rather in sharply declining real wages, widening wage inequality, and reduced working time. Some economists interpret this outcome as a clear and positive sign of considerable flexibility in Russia's new labor market. But labor market flexibility alone cannot account for the labor market outcomes emerging in Russia, and in particular why so much of the decline in output has been absorbed by low wages and work sharing rather than job loss.

The practice of work sharing rather than staff reductions even in unprofitable enterprises with no future reveals how new market relationships are still deeply embedded in older Soviet-style institutional practices. Such responses to sharply declining output have helped to reduce the potential hardship and pain of Russia's Great Depression. But such "soft" employment policies by managers and the government cannot continue indefinitely as enterprise success will increasingly depend on profitability. No wonder so many wage-earners, including those from the former Soviet middle class are ambivalent and confused about the path that market reforms have taken.

6

A New Capitalist Class: Entrepreneurs and the Economic Elite

Prior to 1980 the term *nomenklatura* was almost unknown except as part of the Soviet Communist Party's administrative jargon. By the 1980s the word took on new meaning. As the British historian Eric Hobsbawm points out, the nomenklatura came to symbolize the corruption and ineffiency of the party/state bureaucracy and the cronyism, nepotism, and payments that characterized the Brezhnev "years of stagnation."[1]

But efforts to reform "nomenklatura socialism" did not emerge from the grassroots; they came from the top. For most ordinary people the Brezhnev era signified improving living standards, not stagnation. The initiative for reform came from within the Soviet elite; from among top leaders in the Communist Party who still believed in the possibility of reforming socialism; and from among academics, scientists, experts, and managers who were aware of the need for fundamental economic and political change. Public dissent was, of course, limited and very risky. But criticism pervaded the intellectual and cultural underground and included important sectors of the party and the state.

While Gorbachev wanted to reform elite structures by reducing the power of the Communist Party and the state bureaucracy, free market reformers sought to destroy the power of the political elite by transferring ownership rights and control over state property into private hands. Privatization of state property and the rapid growth of newly created private enterprises have radically changed the economic structure of Russia. Virtually overnight, a new capitalist class has been created through the rapid privatization of state enterprises. This was done before effective rules and institutions regulating their activities were put in place. To secure political support, Russian privatizers, led by Anatolii Chubais, granted concessions to major interest groups— managers, workers, local governments, and the public. It is beyond the scope of this book to review the details of the privatization process.[2] But whatever compromises radical reformers made to hasten the pace of privatization, they believed that by granting privately owned enterprises control over productive assets and cash flow, efficiency would be greatly enhanced and corruption significantly reduced.

To radical reformers the real source of corruption and inefficiency could be traced to the overpoliticized state bureaucracy whose regulatory powers led inevitably to payouts and inefficient decision making. Privatization was aimed at creating a new group of decision makers. In a recent book on privatization in Russia, three advisers to Anatolii Chubais clearly indicate the constituencies free market reformers served. "In Russia . . . free market reformers tend to represent a newly formed political coalition comprised of entrepreneurs, professionals, small business people, and other property owners."[3]

In promoting the interest of a new capitalist class, radical market reformers believed that these new groups would be the key to a more efficient and less corrupt economy. As the evidence in this chapter shows, the new property owners have indeed become the chief beneficiaries of privatization. But have they lived up to the expectations of free market reformers? This is one of the central questions this chapter addresses.

In contrast to the groups whose fate was examined in previous chapters, and whose existence spans the whole of the Soviet and post-Soviet periods, our attention turns to a social group only recently recognized as a legitimate actor—indeed, as a decisive element—in the Russian economy. We focus here on the new Russian *predprinimatel'*—variously rendered as entrepreneur, businessman (woman), business operator. Of course, it is no secret that an "underground" private sector existed in the Soviet past, and in this sense private entrepreneurial activity antedates both the Gorbachev and post-Soviet economic reforms. But in accordance with the general theme of our study, we concentrate here on the business strata whose emergence is associated with the marketization and privatization processes of recent years.

The following are some of the principal questions addressed in this chapter's discussion: How have the new business strata fared economically compared to other socio-occupational strata in Russian society? What are the principal social sources of recruitment of the new business strata? What are the main social components (or social divisions) within the overall business class? Of special interest in this context is the issue of the nature and sources of the upper reaches of the new business class—the post-Soviet economic elite. To what extent has the latter been recruited from "outsiders" rather than from the Soviet nomenklatura and other formerly privileged groups? The available evidence should help shed some light on the larger issue of continuities as well as breaks with the Soviet past.

Conflicting Portraits of a New Social Group— Business Operators

Before turning directly to the specific issues raised in these questions, and to the empirical grounds for our responses to them, we take a brief detour to see how the newly emerging entrepreneurial strata are typically characterized and assessed in the more serious literature on this theme. This route reveals markedly differing and contradictory perceptions and appraisals of these new social groups. These differences do not simply reflect the differing views of "hardliners" (who presumably find it impossible to accept the legitimacy of private entrepreneurship) versus "democrats" (who view a far-reaching private business sector as a necessary condition for the effective functioning of a market economy). The conflicting perceptions of the new social group are drawn exclusively from the pro-reformist literature that shows no nostalgia for the Soviet past.

We begin with the views of the sociologist Tat'iana Zaslavskaia, a respected voice of reform. Her characterization of some of the "deformed features of Russian entrepreneurship," and of the business groups that have gained most from the market-oriented transformations currently under way, paint a highly critical portrait of leading sectors of the emerging business class, one that contrasts quite sharply with the expectations of free market reformers.[4]

> The illicit origins of most of the large-scale and medium-sized capital in the country, the mass corruption of government bodies, the predominance of commercial and financial middleman activity relative to production activity, the feeble legal control over economic activity, and the

spread of racketeering, violent "showdowns" between groups of commercial operators, and terrorist actions have had the result that entrepreneurship has begun to be perceived not only as the most criminal sphere of life but also as a source of the criminalization of the entire society.

Today the Russians who have the best chance of enriching themselves are distinguished not so much by their high level of skills, knowledge, and business energy and talent, as by their possession of advantageous connections, their impudence, and their disdain for the law and for morality. This state of affairs does not correspond to Russians' sociocultural norms and values, and hence is perceived by the majority as a violation of social justice.

These remarks appeared in published form early in 1995, and thus presumably reflect Zaslavskaia's perception of the situation in the early post-Soviet period (1992–94). This point should be recalled when we turn later to illustrations of more positive perceptions of business activity, which stress the advances in business behavior and privatization practices in 1992–94 compared to the final years of Soviet rule.

A portrait of some sections of the business class—indeed, of its most successful strata—that is no less critical than that found in Zaslavskaia's writings appears in the work of the historian and sociologist Evgenii Starikov. In Starikov's view, the "principal accumulator of wealth" in today's Russia is the business stratum that he characterizes as the "comprador bourgeoisie." Its enormous profits are derived mainly from "simple parasitism rooted in intermediary-type operations in the sphere of finance and trade."[5] The themes repeatedly sounded in Starikov's discussion of this leading stratum of the business class are its divorce from the production process, its close links to the state *apparat* and the "gangocracy," and the dependence of its high profits on speculative activity in the foreign exchange and domestic money markets. The "comprador bourgeoisie" and its "entrepreneurial subculture" that Starikov has in mind are, roughly speaking, the Russian equivalent of the leading business strata and their practices "in the former colonial and dependent countries of the third world."[6] The functioning of these groups in the context of market economies was by no means invariably associated with rapid modernization and economic development. Starikov also explicitly recognizes the existence of a Russian "national bourgeoisie" whose activities are associated largely with reliance on "productive" rather than "speculative" capital, and whose entrepreneurial subculture is of a Western or European (rather than "Asiatic") type. But this business stratum seems distinctly less representative of the more successful business groups than the "comprador bourgeoisie."

The literature that stresses a distinctly more favorable portrait of entrepreneurial activity than that found in the writing of Zaslavskaia and Starikov assumes a variety of forms. Sometimes the principal objective appears to be that of accustoming the Russian reader to an unusually positive characterization of the social category of "entrepreneur" or "businessman" and of linking the activities of these groups with the healthy personal qualities of the more "enterprising" and "innovative" members of Russian society. This approach is illustrated in an article by V.G. Smol'kov in a leading Russian sociological journal:

> Today the words "entrepreneur" and "enterprising," cited in the past primarily in the context of the criminal code, have begun to take on a new meaning. Reality has forced us to recognize that among the sources of social and cultural rebirth stand people who have initiative, are business-like, innovative, and think creatively. In the economic sphere that means the entrepreneur.[7]

Some of Smol'kov's discussion is essentially a celebration of those individuals who possess the quality of "enterprise" *(predpriimchivost')*, and thus achieve their goals (whether in the economic sphere or in other areas of social life) through the exercise of "initiative, inventiveness, independence, resourcefulness, non-standard types of decisions, and ultimately a readiness to take risks and bear responsibility for the results."[8] As for those enterprising individuals engaged in the private business sector, Smol'kov's view, not surprisingly, is: "The less the influence of the state on the private sphere, the better."[9] (One cannot help but notice that the habit of celebrating the "leading" role of a particular social group or class in transforming society has remained partially intact in some of the Russian literature, although the subject of the celebration has changed profoundly.)

Not all of the literature that might be loosely characterized as "pro-business" has the simplistic quality reflected in the remarks of Smol'kov cited above. The industrial sociologist Leonid Gordon, for example, whose recent work stresses the positive social role of independent trade unions, directly confronts Starikov's argument concerning the dominant position of "comprador" capital in the post-Soviet economy. Gordon does not question Starikov's description of the prin-

cipal activities of this business stratum, or its frequent links to both the
state and the "gangocracy," but argues that the "comprador bourgeoisie" commonly functions as the precursor or forerunner of a more
normal or productive "national bourgeoisie." "It is enough to look at
the notorious new young dragons in order to see how the compradors
of South Korea, Singapore, Hong Kong and Taiwan have been transformed into entrepreneurs that are now called the national bourgeoisie."[10] Moreover, argues Gordon, business careers that move from
"racketeering" and "financial business" to investment in the production
process are readily observable in today's Russia. Gordon is here expressing the common view that there is something normal about the
early "wild" stage of capitalism that Russia is now experiencing, just as
there is about its ultimate evolution to the more civilized stage that may
be observed in the developed market economies of both East and West.

We conclude our brief review of the contrasting responses to the
emergence of the new entrepreneurial class by examining the views on
this matter of one of the principal architects of early post-Soviet economic reforms—Egor Gaidar. In some respects, Gaidar's relatively
positive portrayal of current entrepreneurial activity (in a volume published in 1995) reflected an approach similar to Gordon's. The latter,
as noted above, did not really celebrate the current activities of dominant business groups, but he did regard them as harbingers of healthier
things to come. Similarly, Gaidar seemed less concerned with spelling
out the specific, positive social functions of the new class of businessmen than with stressing the marked advance they represented compared with the dominant social groups of the immediate past.

Gaidar's sentiments on this matter are expressed with particular
clarity in his contrasting characterization of the social groups that
seemed to symbolize the Soviet past and the market-driven present:

> Let us not forget that the state official is always potentially more crimino-
> genic than the businessman. The businessman can enrich himself honestly,
> if only he is left alone. The state official can enrich himself only dishon-
> estly. Thus the bureaucratic apparatus carries within itself a much
> greater potential for mafia activity than business does. Moreover the
> framework of the bureaucratic (including the punitive) system may
> readily provide a framework for a mafia-like system.[11]

An essentially similar point is made by Gaidar when he contrasts the
economic changes undertaken in 1989–91 with those implemented in

1992–94. The earlier of these periods was marked by the transition to "*nomenklatura* capitalism," with the nomenklatura essentially "looting" what had earlier been state property. The more recent period, although admittedly characterized by sharply declining output and unprecedented inflation, signaled the transition to "semi-democratic" capitalism. In contrast to the past, when "commercial activity" was available to a relatively small number of "selected" individuals, it was now accessible to tens of millions of Russian people.[12] Rather than explicitly celebrating the contributions of an emerging business class to the economic well-being of the Russian population (something that would have seemed obviously premature in 1992–94), Gaidar in effect celebrated the reformist policies that in the near future (in his view) would make it possible for entrepreneurship to ensure a marked improvement in the economic welfare of the Russian masses.

Increasing evidence of corruption and outright criminal behavior of the business elite did not deter the optimism of the leader of Russia's privatization program. In 1994 Anatolii Chubais is reported to have admitted that the new business leaders "steal and steal. . . . They are stealing absolutely everything. . . . But let them steal and take their property. They will then become owners and decent administrators of their property."[13]

By 1996 some radical reformers were no longer so optimistic. Sergei Kovalov, a former dissident and MP for Russia's Choice, the party Chubais helped found, viewed such sentiments as "economic romanticism," a point of view he associated with people who believe that once Russia becomes a market economy, then democracy "and everything good will follow."[14]

The conflicting portrayals of the new business class (or, more accurately, of the anticipated consequences of their activity) by supporters of market reforms suggest some of the difficulties that confront efforts to provide an objective assessment of the new capitalist class. We turn, therefore, to some empirical studies for a closer examination of the new business strata.

Entrepreneurial Strata: Relative Incomes and Sources of Recruitment

Almost everyone agrees that the economic reforms of the early post-Soviet period had a positive impact on the relative economic status of business operators. One measure of the differential impact of these

Table 6.1

Respondents' Views of Changes in Living Standards During "Last Two Years," 1994 (%)

| | Direction of changes in living standards | |
Social group	Increased	Decreased
Entrepreneurs	55.8	26.8
Directors of enterprises	40.9	25.8
Middle-level managerial personnel	40.0	40.0
Pensioners	7.0	76.0
Workers	13.8	65.0
Rural residents	18.2	64.5

Source: Natal'ia Tikhonova, "Russians Are Adapting to the New Conditions of an Unplanned Economy," *Finansovye izvestiia*, October 20, 1994.

Note: This study was conducted by the Russian Independent Institute of Social and National Problems.

reforms on representatives of a variety of social groups is shown in Table 6.1. A survey conducted in mid-1994 by the Russian Independent Institute of Social and National Problems asked representatives of the six social groups shown in Table 6.1 whether their living standards had increased or decreased over the past two years. Only among entrepreneurs and directors of enterprises were the respondents more likely to have experienced an increase than a decrease. The message conveyed by a substantial majority of workers, rural residents, and pensioners was that their living standards had declined over this period, while middle-level managerial personnel were just as likely to have been losers as winners.

Similarly, a study conducted by the Russian Center for Public Opinion Research in mid-1993 pointed to the strikingly different perceptions of the effects of recent economic reforms on the "material positions" of business operators and wage-earners (in both the private and state sectors).[15] Among all five wage-earners' groups distinguished in this study (skilled workers, unskilled workers, white-collar employees, technical specialists, managerial personnel) the proportion of respondents indicating a decline in the "material position" of their families substantially exceeded the proportion experiencing an increase. Exactly the opposite was the case for respondents classified as entrepreneurs—the percentage claiming improved living standards for their families in the past six months was considerably in excess of those who claimed declines.

Of course, such findings are of limited significance. While they do reinforce the impression of a polarization between recipients of wage and business incomes, they tell us nothing of the relative magnitudes of these incomes, and they fail to reveal anything about the substantial differentiation within the business or entrepreneurial strata. Both of these factors will be considered in the sections that follow.

For the moment, we ignore the group commonly characterized as the "economic elite" and focus our attention on business operators mainly involved in relatively small or medium-sized firms. Given the recent emergence of this business stratum, and the fact that serious studies of its composition and activities are at an initial stage, it comes as no surprise that scholars do not always agree on precisely which groups should be included in this social category. Whatever their differences on this score, however, these early studies yield a roughly similar picture of the substantial gap between typical wage and business incomes. Table 6.2 shows the principal groups included by Zaslavskaia in her discussion of the newly emergent "business stratum," and the estimated differential between their incomes and those of wage-earners not engaged in their own business operations.

Two features of Zaslavskaia's treatment of the early post-Soviet business stratum are worth noting. First, this group includes not only the equivalent of full-time business operators engaged in managing their own firms, but also personnel who seek to combine part-time business operations with employment as wage workers or managerial personnel in other firms. Business income in such cases is often essentially a "supplementary" form of income.

The other point worth noting is Zaslavskaia's observation that business incomes (presumably including those serving as the basis for Table 6.2) are often substantially understated.[16] In this light, the approximately threefold average earnings gap[17] between business operators and wage-earners reported in Zaslavskaia's study suggests the prevalence of a more than modest income differential between these social groups. This conclusion seems all the more reasonable when we consider that most of the business operators included in Zaslavskaia's sample were associated with "small enterprises." The pervasive and sizable nature of the income advantages associated with business activity is also suggested by the somewhat surprising observation that "at

Table 6.2

Relative Monthly Incomes of Various Groups of Business Operators in Percentage of Monthly Income of Wage-Earners Not Engaged in Business Activity, May–December 1993

Social groups of income recipients	Relative monthly incomes; Incomes of wage-earners = 100
Business strata	
"Classical entreprenuers"[a]	516
Self-employed[b]	394
Businessmen—managers[c]	401
Part-time entrepreneurs[d]	217
Managers—co-owners[e]	195
Wage-earners not engaged in business activity	100

Source: Tat'iana Zaslavskaia, "The Business Stratum and Russian Society: Essence, Structure, Status," *Obshchestvye nauki i sovremennost'*, 1995, no. 1, p. 31. These figures are based on monthly surveys conducted by the Russian Center for Public Opinion Research.

[a]Owners of mainly small business firms who personally manage the firms they own.

[b]This group is engaged in "individual work activity," that is, the hired labor of outsiders is not employed.

[c]People who combine managerial work in one firm with running their own business in another firm.

[d]People employed as wage workers who are also engaged in business operations of their own.

[e]Hired directors of small and medium-sized joint-stock enterprises who own "substantial proportions of shares" in the firms they manage.

present in Russia, no type of wage work, even the most skilled, brings incomes comparable to the simplest kind of entrepreneurship."[18]

It would be simplistic, of course, to assume that the results of a single sample study conducted by the respected Russian Center for Public Opinion Research provide conclusive evidence of typical income differentials between wage-earners and the new business stratum. If nothing else, the heterogeneous nature of both of these social groups should make us hesitate to characterize such differentials as "typical." But it would be no less foolish to ignore the fact that whatever other studies of the relative incomes of these groups are available to us point to an income gap of a roughly similar and substantial order of magnitude.

This is certainly the case in a study of relative incomes in the city of

Table 6.3

Average Monthly Earnings of Selected Socio-Occupational Groups in City of Nizhnii Novgorod, 1993

Socio-occupational groups	Average monthly earnings (in rubles)
Businessmen[a]	688,485
Wage-earners in state sector	155,352
Wage-earners in private sector	275,650
Managers in state sector[b]	220,698
Managers in private sector[c]	444,243

Source: Vladimir Anurin, "Economic Statification: Attitudes and Stereotypes of Consciousness," *Sotsiologicheskie issledovaniia*, 1995, no. 1, pp. 104–115. The findings are based on a sample survey of 592 persons conducted under the direction of the author at the Volga-Viatsk Cadre Center.

Note: The source used does not specify the period to which these figures apply. But the general context of the discussion suggests that this study was conducted in 1993 or 1994.

[a]This category included persons who identified themselves as "individual owners" or who indicated that their principal activity was that of "independent entrepreneur." It excluded persons who characterized themselves as "co-owners (shareholders)" of an enterprise, or as recipients of "supplementary income" from business activity.

[b]This group is a component of the larger group of "wage-earners in state sector."

[c]This group is a component of the larger group of "wage-earners in private sector."

Nizhnii Novgorod (see Table 6.3) conducted at about the same time as Zaslavskaia's study discussed above. Although the "businessmen" category is defined somewhat differently in these two studies, the sizable income advantage of this social group relative to wage-earners is obvious. In Nizhnii Novgorod, "businessmen's" reported average earnings were more than four times those of wage-earners in the state sector, and more than double the latter group's earnings in the private sector. A Moscow study conducted early in 1993 reinforces the impression that such income differentials between these groups were not unusual. People who "owned their own business" were reported as receiving incomes that were about three and a half times those of wage recipients.[19]

Origins of the New Business Class

What were the principal strata in Soviet and post-Soviet society that served as channels of recruitment to this newly legitimized group of business operators? What kinds of organizational "connections" helped gain access to these relatively high income opportunities in the emerging market economy? Once again, it should be clear that at this point we are not referring to the economic "elite" as such but to the broad range of entrepreneurs or business operators.

Most Russian studies of these issues agree on the principal paths leading to involvement in entrepreneurial activity, even if they differ in assessing their relative importance. There are a variety of ways of describing the relevant channels of recruitment. We identify four such paths.[20]

It is commonly recognized that among the first groups to take advantage of the opportunities created in the late 1980s for legal private entrepreneurship were individuals who had been engaged in "underground" business activity in the immediate pre-perestroika period. Legislation legitimating "individual labor activity" (self-employment) and the organization of "cooperatives" in 1987–88 was among the principal legal vehicles used by former operators in the "shadow" economy to establish what were to be essentially private firms.

The nomenklatura represented a second route to what one Russian scholar characterizes as the "active influx" into business operations. The process began in 1989–90 with the help of "liberated" party and state resources.[21] In the view of another scholar, "the youngest and most capable part of the former nomenklatura" went into entrepreneurial activity.[22] Hence, Russian sources often cite the important role that Komsomol (Young Communist League) functionaries and their organization's financial resources played in the emergence of the new business stratum. Whatever the role of such resources, it is also clear that the "capital of social connections" facilitated the access of state and party/Komsomol functionaries to entrepreneurial opportunities and newly privatized property. However, one of the issues on which Russian scholars disagree is the relative significance of the nomenklatura path to business activity, and hence we return to this issue below.

Former directors of state enterprises constituted a third channel of recruitment of the new business strata. Like other managerial personnel, they frequently used official positions as stepping stones to entrepreneurial activity. Such directors are sometimes treated as a subgroup within the broader party and state nomenklatura, but given their distinctive job positions and the available evidence concerning their important role in the new business stratum (some evidence on this score will be considered below), we treat them as a separate category.

As one commentator puts it (referring to former directors of state enterprises): "It is possible that precisely this group will become the principal backbone of Russian business activity in domestic industry."[23] The success of former "Red Directors" in gaining access to controlling shares of newly privatized enterprises is obviously one of the factors behind this assessment.

Finally, a somewhat heterogeneous group sometimes characterized as "new wave" or "independent" entrepreneurs made their way into new business activity. This group was distinct both from earlier operators in the "shadow" economy and from nomenklatura functionaries. Its most important subgroups have apparently been drawn from the technical and scientific intelligentsia—specialists with a higher education in science, engineering, mathematics, and so on. Indeed, according to at least one study, people with such backgrounds drawn from the Russian Academy of Sciences and the military-industrial complex have made these institutions a significant source of new Russian entrepreneurship.[24] Some ambiguities notwithstanding, studies of the social origins of Russian businessmen almost invariably cite the technical and scientific intelligentsia as a principal source of this new stratum.

Thus, the four groups briefly described above may be viewed as the principal Soviet-era contributors to the post-Soviet Russian business community. In some respects, the groups *not* included as major sources of the new business stratum in Russian studies of this theme are as revealing about the nature of the ongoing process of social transformation as those that *are* included. None of the studies available to us suggest that a significant proportion of the business stratum that emerged in the early post-Soviet period (1992–93) was drawn from workers or peasants. Indeed, the more serious empirical studies suggest that the exact opposite was the case. Table 6.4 shows the job classifications of a sample of Moscow entrepreneurs immediately prior to their entry into private business. Less than 2 percent of these entrepreneurs moved directly into the business world from jobs as workers or collective farmers. More than one-quarter of them were directors of state enterprises, and an additional two-fifths held managerial positions immediately preceding the start of their business careers. If this Moscow study is at all representative, it seems clear that the "lower orders" of Soviet society did not contribute significantly to the emergence of the new business stratum[25]—at least in the late Soviet and immediate post-Soviet periods. While there is some disagreement in the Russian

Table 6.4

Paths to Entrepreneurship: Official Job Status at Last Place of Work Immediately Prior to Entry into Private Business, Moscow Sample, 1992–1993

Official job status	Distribution of business operators by last job (%)
Director of enterprise or institution	26.2
Manager of department of enterprise or institution	41.9
Specialist (with higher education)	25.8
White-collar employee (without higher education)	2.6
Worker, collective farmer	1.9
Never had steady job before entry into business	1.5

Source: V. Radaev, "Russian Entrepreneurs—Who Are They?" *Vestnik statistiki,* 1993, no. 9, p. 7.

Note: These results are based on interviews conducted with 277 chief executives of nonstate entreprises. These interviews were begun sometime in 1992 and completed in April 1993.

literature as to whether a combination of former "shadow operators" and the nomenklatura were the principal sources of the new business stratum, or whether this social function was performed mainly by managerial personnel and an increasingly independent intelligentsia,[26] there can be little doubt that the relationship of workers and peasants to this process was essentially that of "outsiders."

Some additional features of the new business stratum and its activities are worth noting. One such feature concerns the sectors of the economy that seemed particularly attractive to the new entrepreneurial groups. In the Soviet-era language that continued to be used in these discussions, the early post-Soviet business operators flowed mainly into the spheres of "circulation and distribution" rather than into the sphere of "production." In the words of one commentator who sought to sum up the results of a number of empirical studies on this issue, this meant largely "middleman activity, commercial trading operations, stock-exchange operations, and banking."[27] Given the politically unstable and highly inflationary economic environment of this period, it is hardly surprising that sectors with rapid payback of capital and relatively low initial capital requirements were particularly attractive to the new business stratum. Little wonder that "production" (of either capital goods or consumer goods) was largely ignored by these business pioneers in favor of "circulation."

In some respects this business stratum is characterized by a highly unusual, indeed paradoxical, mix of traits. On the one hand, there is something impressive about the relatively high educational attainments of this stratum. One does not normally associate early capitalism with the advanced education of some of its principal agents. However, fully four-fifths of the sample of Moscow entrepreneurs whose pre-entrepreneurial job status is shown in Table 6.4 were college graduates.[28] While there is no basis for accepting such figures as typical of the business stratum as a whole, it should also be recognized that a number of other regional studies conducted in 1992–93 suggest that a sizable proportion of new entrepreneurs—close to 70 percent or more—had completed a higher education.[29] Little wonder that some Russian commentators were prepared to celebrate what seemed to them the implications of such studies: "New Russian business is now the most intellectual in the world."[30]

But some of these studies of Russian entrepreneurs also sounded a very different note, one that seemed difficult to reconcile (at least at first glance) with the image of a highly educated and cultured businessman. The feature we have in mind is best reflected, perhaps, in the concern expressed by a serious scholar in this area that "the development of entrepreneurship in Russia is taking place under conditions quite unfavorable for the formation of a stratum of civilized businessmen."[31] What could possibly block the development of highly educated entrepreneurs (even if one hesitates to accept the "most intellectual in the world" characterization) into "civilized businessmen?"

This expression of concern, of course, is associated with the widely held perception that "Russian business is situated at the edge of the criminal world."[32] Certainly it has not been unusual for business entrepreneurs to forge ties with criminal structures or to engage in bribery of state officials. The evidence on this score is about as clearcut (if not as abundant) as that bearing on the advanced education of entrepreneurs. The findings of a study of entrepreneurship in a city in the Urals, for example, noted the following:

> According to a survey of Cheliabinsk entrepreneurs, 30 out of 40 possessors of large holdings think it is impossible to do business without breaking the law; 90 percent of all respondents are convinced that they cannot engage in business without giving bribes to various state agencies; 65 percent of entrepreneurs have bribed workers in financial auditing bodies; 55 percent have bribed deputies at various levels, 32 percent have

bribed the police, and 27 percent have bribed the courts and the prosecutor's office.[33]

Clearly, highly educated entrepreneurs would not necessarily become "civilized businessmen" in such an environment.

The Business Elite

Given the uncertain nature of the social transformation currently under way in post-Soviet Russia, it seems particularly appropriate to pose the following question. To what extent have the former Soviet-era elites, and the groups close to them, been able to reproduce their power and privileges, albeit in new forms, in post-Soviet society? More specifically—and more in accord with the principal focus of this volume—to what extent have sectors of the former ruling nomenklatura succeeded in gaining access to the ranks of the new business elite? While the material available to us does not permit unambiguous and clear-cut answers to such questions, it certainly can shed some light on them.

What is clear in any case, even to the casual observer, is that the new economic elite has already acquired wealth and material comforts far exceeding those available to the higher levels of the Soviet-era nomenklatura. As Branko Milanovic notes, the privileges of Soviet elites were deliberately concealed and consequently frequently exaggerated by gullible Western analysts.[34] This is no longer the case. As Ol'ga Kryshtanovskaia, a leading expert on the new business elite, observes, "a love of ostentatious glitter and stupifying luxury is a feature inseparable from the Russian *nouveau riche*."[35]

While our principal concern here is with the new economic elites and their channels of recruitment, the sources on which we rely commonly present relevant material on both economic and political elites. Where it seems appropriate to do so, the available findings on both groups will be considered—although this takes us somewhat beyond the "normal" range of issues considered in this volume. In any case, the basic issue being posed here is surely a critical one. Is there persuasive evidence suggesting that a substantial proportion of the principal "winners" emerging in the transition to a post-Soviet society are drawn from the more privileged strata of Soviet society? And if this is, indeed, the case, what aspects of the transition process have facilitated this continuity of elites?

To answer these questions we turn to a number of studies conducted by some of Russia's leading social research institutes in the early 1990s. Obviously, the material on which we draw reflects only the initial findings on this broad theme.

One of the first attempts to confront the issue of the relationship between Soviet and post-Soviet elites was undertaken in a study conducted at the Russian Center for Public Opinion Research by Natal'ia Ershova.[36] Among her principal tasks, Ershova traced the changing fortunes of a sample of the Soviet "ruling elite" (presumably including leading party and state functionaries) between the late 1980s and the early post-Soviet years. Ershova's findings suggest a rather high rate of reproduction of elite status during this period. "More than 60 percent of the representatives of the former nomenklatura today still occupy elite positions comparable to the nomenklatura posts of the Soviet period."[37] This statement was made by Ershova at a scholarly conference held in December 1993, and thus presumably applied to the situation prevailing after close to two years of the post-Soviet era. Moreover, Ershova noted that another 15 percent of the sample representing the Soviet "ruling elite" now held positions very close to current elite status ("just one step below the elite level narrowly defined"). Thus, if we are guided by Ershova's findings, it would appear that fully three-quarters of Soviet-era party and state officialdom retained the equivalent of "elite" or "near-elite" socioeconomic status some two years into the post-Soviet period. The remaining segment of Ershova's nomenklatura sample was either receiving a pension in retirement (11 percent) or was simply "outside the circle of those holding leading positions today" (13 percent).[38] In any case, the continuity of elite status appears considerable. But what does elite (or near-elite) status mean in the post-Soviet period in the context of Ershova's study? What socio-occupational groups are involved?

Our review of Ershova's study thus far is based on her findings concerning the fate of a group she characterizes as a sample of the Soviet "ruling elite" or, quite simply, as the "former nomenklatura"—a group presumably including leading party and state officials. But at a certain point Ershova asks what happened to a group she characterizes as the "purely party nomenklatura." Whether this is a distinct, somewhat narrower Soviet elite group than the ones referred to earlier (i.e., the "ruling elite," the "former nomenklatura") is not altogether clear. But once again, Ershova's report on the fate of the "purely party nomenklatura" suggests that the more powerful and well-to-do groups of Soviet society largely retained their privileged status during the early years of post-Soviet rule. What is more, Ershova indicates here—albeit in rather broad terms—the types of positions the former party nomenklatura tended to acquire in the post-Soviet period. "One third of the Party nomenklatura is today at the top level of state administration, while another third occupies command positions in the economy."[39] Moreover, once again, if current near-elite positions are considered (the "second echelon" of the elite), then fully four-fifths of Ershova's sample of the former party nomenklatura held relatively privileged (elite or near-elite) positions two years after the dissolution of the Soviet Union.

Little wonder that Ershova repeatedly affirms the relevance of the concept of "reproduction of elites" in the face of the marketization process and the significant changes in political institutions that have affected Russian society. But the sense in which this concept is used must be clearly understood. For Ershova it means essentially that there is substantial overlapping of old and new elites, that significant segments of the Soviet-era ruling elite and groups close to it have retained high-level economic and/or political status in the early post-Soviet period—a period of significant decline in the living standards of much of the Russian population. But it does not mean that the post-Soviet elite—however defined—is a simple replica of the Soviet-era elite. Indeed, Ershova makes it clear that those members of the post-Soviet elite who were associated with private business enterprise in 1992–93 were much less likely to have their roots in the Soviet ruling elite than those who still functioned in the state sector.[40]

A recent study of local elites in Altai Territory by the sociologist Vladimir Shubkin also suggests that along with significant continuities between old and new (political and economic) elites, some segments of the "new Russians" appear to have attained their current high positions (in the economy in this case) independently of any obvious links with the former Soviet nomenklatura. Table 6.5 displays some rather revealing characteristics of the groups characterized by Shubkin as post-Soviet political and economic elites in this territory on the basis of a study conducted in 1993–94.

The political elites are essentially local representatives of the executive and legislative branches of government. The economic elites—

Table 6.5

**Background Characteristics of Local "Ruling Elite,"[a] Altai
Territory, 1993–1994**

Types of elites	Percentage with higher education	Percentage of former members of CPSU	Percentage included in nomenklatura of Central Committee and Territorial Committee of CPSU[b]
Political elite:			
Local representatives of executive branch of government	100	95	35
Local representatives of legislative branch of government	100	95	26
Economic elite:			
Chief executives of large state enterprises and of joint-stock companies in which state has controlling share	100	78	66
Chief executives of large nonstate enterprises	100	0	0

Source: Vladimir N. Shubkin, "Ruling Elites of Siberia (Based on Material for Altai Territory)," *Sotsiologicheskii zhurnal*, 1995, no. 1, p. 150.

[a]This is the characterization applied by the director of the Altai study.

[b]This presumably applies to individuals who held positions in the Soviet period, appointment to which required approval by the Central or Territorial Committee of the Communist Party.

who are of greater interest to us—include two groups: (a) chief executives of "the largest" state enterprises and of joint-stock companies in which the state held a controlling interest, and (b) chief executives of "large" nonstate enterprises. What is clear is that substantial proportions of the political elites of 1993–94 and of the top management of state-connected firms in those years had been closely associated with the ruling strata of the Soviet era. Thus, more than 90 percent of the post-Soviet local political elite and more than three-quarters of the directors of state-connected economic enterprises had been Communist Party members in the Soviet period. Moreover, sizable proportions of these new local elites had previously been included in the nomenklatura of the central and territorial committees of the Soviet Communist Party (especially the heads of state enterprises, two-thirds of whom had attained nomenklatura status in the Soviet era). Clearly, having one's roots in the former ruling party was by no means an obstacle to the attainment of elite status in the post-Soviet period—at least for three of the four groups distinguished in Table 6.5.

What is surprising and surely somewhat unusual is that none of the members of the group identified by Shubkin as the new economic elite in the nonstate sector—"businessmen"—in Table 6.5 had any connection with the ruling party in the Soviet period. Indeed, the only characteristic that this elite group shared with other elements of the post-Soviet elite was a relatively high level of education. That there was room at the top for "outsiders" or "newcomers" in the early post-Soviet period seems clear from Ershova's work as well as other studies. But the complete disconnection between the new private business elite and the ruling elite of the Soviet period as portrayed in Table 6.5 for Altai Territory can hardly be regarded as typical. Other studies to be discussed shortly (as well as that already presented) suggest a somewhat closer relationship between Soviet and post-Soviet elites. However, the findings shown in Table 6.5 reflect the work of a serious Russian scholar and cannot be ignored, although Shubkin does not claim that they represent a situation common in Russian society.

Perhaps the most ambitious study of the changing characteristics of elite strata—covering the Brezhnev, Gorbachev, and early Yeltsin eras—was undertaken by the sociologist Ol'ga Kryshtanovskaia. Her findings reveal significant changes in the demographic and social characteristics of ruling groups over this period. Some of the most important changes in the composition of elite strata as we move from the Brezhnev era through the Gorbachev years and into the Yeltsin period clearly point to the "modernization" and "professionalization" of elite groups. These changes may be briefly summarized as follows:[41] (a) a decline in the average age of elite strata; (b) a decline in the proportion of the elite of rural origin; (c) an increase in the proportion of the elite with advanced academic degrees; (d) an increase in the proportion of those whose higher education involved specialization in economics or jurisprudence (and a decline in the proportion majoring in engineering, agriculture, or military technology); and particularly important, (e) an increase in the proportion of those attaining elite status without following the normal nomenklatura path.

While these are significant changes, and at least in some respects obviously reflect the reformist policies of both the Gorbachev and Yeltsin governments, one aspect of Kryshtanovskaia's findings not included in the above summary deserves special attention, given the principal theme of this volume. We refer to her findings concerning the elite stratum she characterizes as the "business elite." This group includes "the heads of the largest banks, exchanges, and industrial-financial groups in the country,"[42] and the general context of Kryshtanovskaia's discussion suggests that her findings in this area apply to 1993. (More recent empirical studies, although less extensive and systematic, essentially reinforce her findings.)[43] Here we essentially repeat the questions posed earlier: To what extent was the post-Soviet business elite (this time based on Kryshtanovskaia's all-Russia sample) of this period drawn from the former party/state nomenklatura? To what extent was movement into this new stratum open to "outsiders"? The answers to these questions, suggested by Kryshtanovskaia's findings, may be observed in Table 6.6. This table also sheds some light on the extent of continuity between the political elites of the early Yeltsin era and the nomenklatura of the final years of Soviet rule.

It seems clear from this material that the attainment of elite status— whether in economic or political form—was significantly dependent on a nomenklatura background. Thus, more than 60 percent of the early Yeltsin-era business elite was drawn from the party/state elite (the nomenklatura) of the late Soviet period. Ershova's concept of the "reproduction of elites" is certainly applicable here, and even more so to some categories of the political elite identified by Kryshtanovskaia. Thus, three-quarters of President Yeltsin's immediate entourage and the members of the central Russian government, as well as more than four-fifths of leading regional government executives (the "regional elite"), were drawn from the former nomenklatura.

But caution is needed lest we exaggerate the degree of "reproduction of elites." While the bulk of the new business and political elites were clearly drawn from the former nomenklatura, they were drawn mainly from what Kryshtanovskaia characterizes as its "second and third ranks," rather than from its highest levels. Thus, while more than 60 percent of the new business elite had followed the nomenklatura path, only 5 percent of this elite group had reached its highest levels (see Table 6.6). In other words, the Yeltsin-era business elite was more likely to be drawn from former local Komsomol functionaries and

Table 6.6

Proportion of Yeltsin-era [a] Business and Political Elites Drawn from Former Nomenklatura: Kryshtanovskaia Study

| | Proportion recruited from former nomenklatura | |
Elite strata	Percentage from nomenklatura as a whole	Percentage from top-level nomenklatura[b]
Business elite	61.0	5.0
Presidential entourage[c]	75.0	24.2
Party elite[d]	57.1	35.0
Members of Russian government	74.3	15.4
Regional elite	82.3	8.9
Total, elite sample	69.9	17.7

Source: Ol'ga Kryshtanovskaia, "The Tranformation of the Old Nomenklatura into the New Russian Elite," *Obshchestvennye nauki i sovremennost'*, 1995, no. 1, p. 65.

[a]These figures appear to apply mainly to 1993.

[b]This applies to persons holding positions that were formerly subject to ratification by the Politburo or the Secretariat of the CPSU Central Committee.

[c]This refers to "leading members of the President's apparatus, his advisers, and members of the President's Council."

[d]This refers to leaders of the largest Russian political parties in 1993.

upper-level managerial personnel than from leading party and state officials of the Soviet period—although the latter were certainly not absent in the new business elite. The other point worth noting here—however obvious it may be—is that while nomenklatura status was clearly an advantage in adapting successfully to the business opportunities offered by post-Soviet society, it was by no means a necessary condition for entry into the new business or political elites. More than one-third of leading businessmen[44] and a significant proportion of the post-Soviet political elite (although clearly a minority of this group) made it to the "top" without following a nomenklatura career ladder.

Nonetheless, judging by the bulk of the evidence reviewed above, it seems clear that substantial elements of the ruling stratum of Soviet society were able to retain their power and privileges in the post-Soviet period. Indeed, since it was the nomenklatura (however divided this group became) that implemented the reform process in both the Gorbachev and Yeltsin periods, it should come as no surprise to learn that some elements of this group had a "head start" in the struggle for access to the newly emerging elite positions in both the economic and political spheres.

Since our concern here is mainly with the new business elite, a brief review of some aspects of the privatization process in both its unofficial (pre-1992) and official forms should help reveal some of the mechanisms that facilitated the movement of sections of the former ruling stratum to positions of leadership in the new private business sector.

While the nomenklatura had long had access to consumption opportunities and services that were not generally available to the bulk of the population, the years of perestroika witnessed the emergence and increasing importance of a new variety of nomenklatura privileges, namely, entry into profit-making activity via commercial operations. Various groups of the nomenklatura became involved in the creation of joint ventures with foreign firms, in real estate operations (for example, by leasing out space in relatively well maintained party buildings), and in access to export-import operations not available to less well-placed groups. Involvement in such operations was clearly facilitated by the availability of credit at preferential interest rates ("and sometimes without any interest at all") to some nomenklatura groups.[45]

A revealing summary of some key elements of the privatization process during perestroika by Kryshtanovskaia suggests that there were solid empirical grounds for the popular phrase commonly used to characterize this process—"nomenklatura privatization":

> Whereas formerly, property was at the disposal but not in the possession of the nomenklatura, it now became legally defined property. A minister became the holder of controlling shares in a concern; an administrative head in the Ministry of Finance became the president of a commercial bank; a senior manager in Gossnab [the former Soviet agency responsible for distributing the "means of production"] became the chief executive of the stock exchange. Of course, independent, random personages were also drawn into the process of privatization . . . and many of these achieved success in their new careers. But the main conclusion is that the process of reforming the economy took place under the direct control of the nomenklatura.[46]

The nature and ultimate consequences of the official privatization process begun in 1992 is a large theme that we do not undertake to study here. But it does seem appropriate to point to some of the evidence suggesting that in its early stages official privatization—at the very least—did not reverse or undo the process of reproduction of elite status noted above for substantial segments of the former nomenklatura. Thus, the findings cited earlier of Ershova and Kryshtanovskaia, both of which provide persuasive evidence of considerable continuity of elites, apply to the situation prevailing a year or more after the initiation of official privatization. Also worth noting are the results of a poll conducted in September 1994 by the Russian Center for Public Opinion Research (VTsIOM) some two years after the initiation of official privatization. People employed at privatized firms (and some firms in the process of privatization) were asked who "really owns" (or "will own") their enterprises. While the responses differed somewhat depending on occupational position, fully two-thirds of all respondents answered by citing the "current director" or "current management."[47] Such responses were much more frequent than the invocation of "the work collective" or "the shareholders' meeting." Clearly, the groups typically perceived as "real" owners—plant directors and senior management personnel—were quite likely to have been drawn from the ranks of the nomenklatura or from groups close to it. Finally, it should be recognized that the perception of post-Soviet privatization as a process that facilitated the access of Soviet-era elites to leading positions in the new business class was a view widely shared by the democratically oriented intelligentsia.[48]

Of course, there are some scholars who regard the views we have summarized above as exaggerating the role of the nomenklatura in the new business elite. But it is striking that such skeptics seem to agree with the view that lies at the very core of the position taken by those who regard "nomenklatura capitalism" as an appropriate way of characterizing the system that has emerged in the post-Soviet period: "[T]he development of powerful financial and industrial empires is impossible unless close relationships are formed with the state."[49]

The common career paths followed by large segments of those identified as political and economic elites in the post-Soviet period certainly did not hurt the development of the kind of "empires" referred to in the above statement. As for the nature of the close relationships between key state functionaries and representatives of the economic elite commonly observed by Russian scholars, they essentially took the form of an exchange process in which state officials would sell their "services" for a price. The "services" might include granting a license to engage in certain commercial operations, the leasing of state premises, or the granting of credit on favorable terms. The selling price of these "services" might involve a share of the company's profits, a position as stockholder or founder of the firm, or quite simply a direct bribe. The essential point is that a considerable number of official state positions, as well as productive property formerly owned by the state, underwent a process of "privatization."[50]

A particularly striking illustration of this exchange process was reported at the end of 1996 in the *Financial Times*.[51] According to this article, top-level government positions were awarded to some prominent members of the economic elite in exchange for substantial financial and media support for Boris Yeltsin's presidential campaign. The report notes that in early 1996 a small group of some of the most successful businessmen met regularly with Anatolii Chubais to help revive Yeltsin's then fading political fortunes and help shape Kremlin policy. Two members of the group were ultimately appointed deputy secretary of the Security Council and first deputy prime minister for the economy.

At the beginning of this chapter we posed the question whether the new economic elite is living up to the expectations of free market reformers. The answer seems clear. Thus far, the evidence suggests that Russia's new capitalists have yet to follow patterns of behavior that inform some of the basic assumptions of the free market theory of privatization. History, culture, and institutional constraints continue to undermine radical reformers' assumptions about capitalist behavior.

7

Why No Social Democracy in Russia?

Unlike other capitalist countries, Russia started its transition to a modern market system as a state-controlled industrial economy and not as an economy characterized by early unbridled capitalism. Rather than humanizing an already existing capitalist system by increasing the role of government, trade unions, and other voluntary associations, Russia needed to dismantle its state-controlled economy and replace it with a modern mixed economy. While this was no simple task, the presence of an independent labor movement and a government prepared to undertake appropriate "social regulations" and "social protection" promised to make the transition to a more civilized market economy at least a realistic possibility. Most reformers understood that this historical undertaking would entail changing Russia's extensive social and economic security system and that this in turn would inevitably lead to some increases in economic insecurity and inequality. But as we noted in chapter 5, they thought that such costs would be a small price to pay to move Russia toward a market economy of the type found in most Western capitalist democracies.

As the preceding chapters have demonstrated, the sort of capitalism emerging in Russia is not what most Russians had envisioned. The unfolding market system has exhibited more of the attributes of nineteenth-century capitalism than of contemporary welfare states. Nor was this accidental. Reformers in the Yeltsin government believed that labor and social welfare issues should not be a primary policy concern. When Aleksandr Shokhin, then secretary of labor, assured an adviser to the Gaidar team in 1991 that "there would be no talk of social democracy but (only) of real liberalism," he signaled that economic policy would not be guided by popular anxieties about economic and social insecurity.[1]

As reform unfolded and social distress increased, Russians became increasingly disaffected and alienated from the reform process and the pain that it inflicted on the population. VTsIOM, the highly respected public polling research center, has monitored this dramatic shift in the population's support for capitalism.[2] Of those surveyed in 1993, 81 percent favored a system based on private property and market relationships. Only 7 percent thought that an economy regulated by state planning was better. By May 1995 Russians were no longer certain. Only 22 percent said they favored a capitalist economy, while the remainder were evenly divided between those who thought state planning was better (39 percent) and those who were uncertain (39 percent).

But this did not mean that Russians wanted the reform process to end. Of those surveyed in 1995, 73 percent thought that market reforms were necessary. Only 27 percent wanted the process stopped. What they did oppose was the current direction of the reform process. Fifty percent of those questioned thought that market reforms should provide people with adequate social protection. The overwhelming majority (77 percent) were critical of the new economic elites who, they thought, were only interested in making as much money as possible and who paid little attention to the concerns of the larger society. While they did not wish to return to the kind of life that existed in the USSR before 1985, they disliked the growing disparity between the rich and the poor that Russian capitalism was exhibiting. In short, when asked what they thought the Russian road to capitalism should look like, their vision closely resembled the social democratic attributes of modern welfare states.*

This raises some puzzling questions. Why have Russians been unable to implement their image of social and economic reform? Why is it that a social democratic path to a market economy was not taken in a country where so many elements of social democracy were already in place?

---

*We use the term social democracy to mean a regulated market system that includes mixed forms of property ownership, provides an array of protective measures and institutions to reduce economic insecurity, and uses taxes and subsidies to promote greater equality of opportunity and results. As a political philosophy, social democracy endorses socialist values in the economy and the ideals of liberal democracy in political and social affairs.

Answers to these questions raise larger issues about the nature of the Soviet transition to capitalism. In what sense can the social transformation under way in post-Soviet society be legitimately called a "revolution," and in what sense does this characterization seem inappropriate? The rapid and dramatic changes certainly had some of the appearances of a revolution. The party/state bureaucracy that controlled the economy and society has collapsed. Although market institutions are still underdeveloped, markets have replaced central planning as the primary regulator of economic decisions, and most enterprises are now either partially or fully privatized. Russia has become a more open society with more limited state control over its citizens. These outcomes are indeed revolutionary.

But the word "revolution" does not adequately capture the why and for whom of the transformation. The paradoxical outcomes of who is winning and who is losing suggest that a different process is under way. In our view, the collapse of the Soviet Union and the transformation of Russian society are part of a devolutionary rather than a revolutionary process. This distinction provides a better way of understanding the continuities as well as the changes in Russia's particular road to capitalism, and helps explain why social democracy has had little opportunity to take root in Russia.

Devolution suggests the disintegration of the social order rather than its revolutionary transformation. As the political scientist Theda Skocpol points out, revolutions are "accompanied by and are in part carried through class-based revolts from below."[3] This did not occur in Russia. Power dissolved more by default than by revolutionary upheaval. The few thousand who stood with Yeltsin during those dramatic days that "shook the world" revealed much about confusion and conflict among the old elite and provided little evidence of decisive action by a broad-based movement from below to overthrow the established social system. In a devolution, unlike a revolution, power is transformed from above but the old elite is not destroyed. As the evidence in chapter 6 suggests, many of the old elite continue to survive on the remains of changing institutional structures while they seek to sustain and advance their interests during the period of reconstruction. The devolutionary process is vividly described by Russians as resembling "a sudden shotgun blast that causes all the crows to fly up out of the tree, hover for a time to look around, and then quietly resettle, though sometimes on different branches."[4]

The first shotgun blast occurred in the old Soviet Union in the mid-1980s. By then it was becoming increasingly clear to some that the communist leadership could no longer delay economic reforms. But real reform could not be implemented unless the corruption, opportunism, and inefficiency of the party/state bureaucracy were broken. The essence of Gorbachev's reform strategy was to weaken the Communist Party's control over the government and economy and to make elected government representatives more accountable to the voters. As president, Gorbachev moved boldly to dismantle the cumbersome ministerial planning system and give enterprises greater autonomy and responsibility in economic decision making.

Gorbachev's efforts to create some variant of market socialism met resistance from the nomenklatura who, in pursuit of their own interests, sought to take advantage of the loosening party/state direction over decision making. But the substantial diffusion of administrative controls to regional and local levels took place before effective and legitimate economic and political institutions were in place to help regulate and coordinate economic and political decisions. The radical programs embodied in the 400– and 500–day economic plans were urgent attempts to overcome the crisis in the production and distribution of goods and services.

In the power struggle that unfolded, Boris Yeltsin used the rapid devolution of the Soviet Union and shock therapy to hasten the collapse of the communist-controlled command system. Yeltsin finished what Gorbachev had perhaps unwittingly begun. While Gorbachev tried vainly to introduce a more democratic socialist economy, in the end the conflict between the Gorbachev and the Yeltsin forces was part of a longer historical process that weakened and finally destroyed communist-state direction of the economy and society. The devolutionary process that ensued ended Gorbachev's hope of creating some variant of democratic socialism. But in further weakening the effectiveness and authority of the state, it also inhibited the development of a more socially responsible society.

Social democratic reform depends on the commitment and capacity of government to implement policies that redirect resources to losing groups so they can be protected against market failures. In Russia, the state has been unable and unwilling to reduce social distress and inequality in the distribution of income and wealth. Although in 1991 it was common for democratically oriented reformers to support the replacement of state socialism by a social democratically oriented market system, the implementation of free market reforms not only undermined the development of a social democratic reform strategy, but also weakened the state's capacity to reduce social distress and inequality.

The fragility of the state bureaucracy and the devolution of political and economic power to regional and local authorities has reduced the capacity of the state to collect taxes and support social programs. Businesses and citizens avoid paying taxes, and corruption has become commonplace. This is particularly problematic for policy makers trying to enforce stricter financial and fiscal constraints on government agencies and enterprises. Without sufficient revenue, government must restrict spending on desperately needed social programs and services. Without central government support, local authorities and enterprises lack the financial resources to fulfill their obligations to citizens.

Nor has the diffusion of government authority eliminated the legacy of corruption and opportunism among government bureaucrats and business. Stories of such abuse are legion. The authors have witnessed firsthand how former high-level officials (now businessmen) used their old connections with local officials to gain access to government resources and wealth. The market has not ended the culture of corruption and cronyism that was commonplace under communism. But today the economic rewards for such behavior are much greater and the punishment less severe. In this environment, criminal organization and corrupt business practices have become pervasive.

The declining effectiveness of government and the erosion of confidence in it has another consequence. It contributes to fears of impending social disorder and moves people to be more cautious about changing the course of reform. Anxiety about looming disaster partly helps explain the surprising passivity of the intelligentsia in the face of hardships imposed by radical reform, and is another important reason for the weakness of social democracy in Russia.

The relative silence of the formerly critical voices of the intelligentsia is puzzling because they played a decisive role in toppling the Soviet system at a time when the consequences of such activity were far more uncertain. During the Gorbachev period many had been strong advocates of democratic socialism. But after communism fell, market socialism and soon even social democracy became tainted with the stamp of the past. Support for such programs among the intelligentsia waned, as many saw them as utopian or, worse, a path back to communism.

Professionals from the "mass intelligentsia" (teachers, doctors, scientists, and so forth) have not been spared declines in living standards. As Chapters 3 and 5 suggest, many have fallen into poverty. But despite the intelligentsia's disappointments with their own deteriorating living conditions and with growing inequality, corruption, and criminality among the economic and political elite, they remain wary of shifting the course of the transition. Changing the direction of reform often evokes tragic visions of precipitating social disorder and the return to some form of authoritarianism. Fear of chaos is understandable in a society whose historical memory since 1917 has been shaped by two world wars, a civil war, and millions of casualties of Stalinist economic miscalculations and terror. Consequently, many of the intelligentsia believe that there is no alternative but to endure this period of trouble and misfortune.

Yeltsin and his advisers effectively played on those anxieties during the presidential contest with the Communist Party candidate, Gennadi Zyuganov. Controlling the media and promising to ease social distress, Yeltsin repeatedly warned that a communist victory would mean a return to the economic shortages of the communist era or even worse, the Gulag. Yet, even some of Yeltsin's strongest supporters were becoming disenchanted with what they saw as the "corrupt big business interests dominating the Yeltsin and Chernomyrdin teams."[5] Some Western political scientists and Russian specialists analyzing the election believed that Zyuganov was serious about moving Russia in a social democratic direction and that he had the capacity to do so.[6] In the end, however, Zyuganov, unlike his Polish counterpart, Aleksander Kwasniewski, could not distance himself from some of his more orthodox constituencies, who traditionally regarded social democracy as a betrayal of genuine socialism. Consequently, Zyuganov was unable to project to the Russian people the image of his party as a reformed social democratic movement. The Yeltsin election strategy worked.

But fear of disorder does not fully explain why more of the intelligentsia have not taken up the mantle of social democratic reform. An equally important reason for their passivity has been the absence of effective institutions that could nurture a social democratic alternative to economic reform. In developed market systems, workers and their organizations have been the major agents promoting social democratic change. Recent experiences of many developed market economies suggest that without such a base of support, voices for social democratic reform have difficulty being heard. Rather than fostering the growth of a strong independent labor movement, the devolutionary process in Russia has exposed the weaknesses of workers and their organizations. This more than any other factor helps explain why social democracy has played such a limited role in the evolution of capitalism in Russia.

During the Soviet era, trade unions' ties to the Communist Party and management undermined their role as representatives of worker interests. Soviet planning and communist ideology fostered worker–management dependency. Relatively low wages under conditions of artificially created labor shortages limited managerial control over work discipline. But workers were also dependent on managers and trade unions for a variety of social and human services. Social relations within the enterprise had been designed to encourage collective identification with the firm and to discourage worker mobility. Until Gorbachev opened up Soviet society, workers could not form independent trade unions. In exchange for political compliance, workers received job security, low but gradually rising real wages, and a broad array of socialized human services, many of which were beyond the reach of the most organized labor movements in the West. This implicit social contract that exchanged social security and a relatively high level of equality for political quiescence stimulated the development of a passive and dependent working class.[7]

Since the fall of communism, greater labor market flexibility has not broken working-class dependency on management. The emergence of a large labor surplus has undermined whatever power workers may have had in the workplace. Many workers still count on the social and human services provided by their enterprises. Given the large pool of redundant labor and very low unemployment benefits, workers are worried about losing their jobs and have until recently been unwilling to engage in labor actions that threaten their firms' financial stability.

Yet managers continue to employ more workers than they need to produce a sharply diminished output. As we suggested in Chapter 5, there are many reasons for this. Workers have accepted lower real wages and reduced working time in exchange for employment. Relatively low wages, high severance pay, and, until recently, an excess wage tax[8] have reduced the financial incentives to dismiss workers. Privatization has also played a role in inhibiting dismissals. Managers have used workers' support to enhance their control of the enterprise and prevent outside takeovers. But many managers also continue to feel a strong social obligation to protect their workers' jobs.[9]

As a consequence, a new implicit social contract between workers and managers has emerged. Constrained by the high cost of job loss, workers accept pay cuts and more flexible work time in exchange for continuing employment. Thus far, most workers have experienced the economic costs of reform primarily through sharply lower real wages and reduced hours of work. But this accommodation between workers and managers is highly unstable and may crumble under the strain of tighter budgets and the enforcement of bankruptcy laws.

In this economic environment the potential for developing a strong independent labor movement is very limited. During 1989–91, increased labor militancy, especially by the newly formed Independent Trade Union of Miners (NGP),[10] seemed to signal the birth of a new movement for social democracy in the Soviet Union. But the new unions have stagnated in the post–communist period. Many of their most talented leaders have left to pursue positions in new business enterprises.

The new unions' relationship with the government accounts for some of their difficulties. Before the collapse of communism, independent unions took to the streets in opposition to the government and in support of Yeltsin. When Yeltsin assumed power they dropped their adversarial relationship to government. This put them in a contradictory position. On the one hand, they continued to proclaim their militancy in defense of workers' living standards. On the other hand, trade union leaders and their intellectual advisers, fearful that worker militancy might destabilize the government and the reform process, remained relatively passive in the face of economic policies that sharply reduced the economic position of workers. As a result, most workers believe that the independent unions are unresponsive to rank-and-file distress.

Without the realization of an effective independent labor movement, labor politics has not been a force for social democracy. Instead, it continues to repeat older patterns of labor relations. The Federation of Independent Trade Unions of Russia (FNDR), the successor of the former communist-led confederation, is still the largest worker organization. At the end of 1991 the Yeltsin government tried to promote a social partnership between labor and management by establishing a consultative Trilateral Commission to review social and economic policies. The government hoped that by involving the parties in the reform process and mediating differences between labor and management, potential social conflicts could be reduced. The Trilateral Commission never fulfilled its mission. Faced with plant closings and the specter of massive unemployment, the FNDR joined with employer associations to demand credits and subsidies to support their ailing industries.[11] Fearing a social explosion, the government usually acceded to their demands until 1994.

But increasing pressures from new private businesses and domestic and international financial institutions insisting on stricter budgetary and financial control have begun to crack the alliance between unions and employers. Since 1994, financial stabilization has been more rigorously implemented. Employers faced with declining demand and increased credit constraints have responded by delaying wage payments and reducing work time.[12] Unions both old and new have begun to stage short strikes, directed mainly at the government, demanding back pay. The number of strikes has risen sharply, from 514 in 1994 to 8,856 in 1995.[13] A massive strike by 500,000 miners in February 1996 signaled the fragility of labor peace. But labor is extremely weak and vulnerable and many workers are disillusioned with market reform. These feelings of alienation were captured by a miner just before the December 1995 parliamentary elections: "I put my faith in a new ideology," he said. "If we have learned anything in this land, you would think it was that no ideology will ever help the common man."[14]

Social Democracy vs. Authoritarianism

The frailty of labor peace suggests that the divisions between winners and losers continue to pose a threat to political and social stability. In a society where increasing numbers of Russians feel excluded from the process of change, the possibility of a social explosion cannot be ruled out. Not surprisingly, when Russians were asked in early 1996 whether "order or democracy was more important for Russia now," only 9 percent chose democracy.[15] In a period of devolution the desire for order is understandable, but under such circumstances people are more likely to be manipulated by groups seeking authoritarian solutions rather than democratic ones.

Confusion with and disaffection from market reforms is exacerbated by another important aspect of the devolutionary process: the breakdown of important social symbols and values. Unlike the great revolutions of the past, the discredited ideology of Soviet communism has not given birth to a more compelling sense of purpose toward which society is moving. The idea of an open society—the appeal to freedom from the oppressive constraints of the state—is an important force for modernization.[16] But it does not answer the question, Freedom for what?

In a society where egalitarian norms have been highly valued, negative freedom alone cannot define the aims of liberty.[17] The absence of a larger vision of freedom may be problematic for a society building a new market system. As early as 1922, John Maynard Keynes, one of the most important contributors to the development of the modern welfare state, dismissed the appeal of communism but warned that "unless men are united by a common aim or moved by objective principles, each one's hand will be against the rest and the unregulated pursuit of individual advantage may soon destroy the whole."[18] Those prophetic words apply to post–communist Russia. If Russia turns away from democracy, it may be because its concept of freedom is too narrow.

Radical reformers have focused almost exclusively on the negative aspects of freedom. They thought that by removing counterproductive state regulations they could enhance efficiency and choice and eliminate onerous bureaucratic privileges and corruption. But lifting the constraints on freedom has not increased the capacity of most Russians to lead the life they would like to live. As we noted at the beginning of this book, being "free to choose" requires both negative and positive freedoms. Declining living standards, social and economic insecurity, and growing inequality have greatly diminished the capacity of Russians to choose the life they value. To enhance overall freedom, government must play a positive role in reducing those impediments to freedom. Valuing both negative and positive freedom has ethical implications as well, because as the economist Amartya Sen argues, it involves people in both the duty to help others when their negative rights are threatened and the duty to help others in their capacity to achieve the life they value.[19]

Radical economic reform in Russia has paid little attention to the positive principles of freedom. The focus on financial stabilization and rapid privatization has undermined living standards and increased inequality and insecurity. Inflation has finally diminished, but the cost has been a continuing decline in both aggregate production and real wages, which are now more than 50 percent below their pre-reform levels. As we noted in Chapter 2, financial constraints have reduced spending on health and social services. Partly as a result, the number of deaths increased by approximately 40 percent between 1990 and 1995, a total rise of almost 1,700,000 people.[20]

Recently, some prominent Russians, joined by five U.S. Nobel prize–winning economists, strongly criticized the direction of market reform and presented a social democratic alternative. They argued that a workable market system requires an active role by government to reduce the criminalization of the economy, strengthen market institutions, promote competition, and stimulate economic growth. They proposed that Russia introduce a new social contract "to ensure that the benefits of the new economic order are shared." And they advocated "restoring health care, education and a humane level of social support services." They also suggested that "a well-enforced system of progressive taxation could finance public needs and redress widening economic inequality."[21] But such proposals have limited possibilities of implementation in the current political and economic environment.

One factor, however, has not changed: the increasing divide between winners and losers in the transition to capitalism. Growing inequality and insecurity are the seeds of social disorder. The real battle for democracy in Russia is no longer between communism and capitalism. Russia's newly won freedoms are threatened by the growing divisions between winners and losers. Without greater attention to social democratic reforms, the specter of authoritarianism will continue to haunt Russia's fragile experiment with capitalism.

Notes

Notes to Chapter 1

1. There is extensive literature on negative and positive freedom. See, for example, Isaiah Berlin, *Four Essays on Liberty* (Oxford: Oxford University Press, 1969); Amartya K. Sen, "Markets and Freedom," The Development Economics Research Programme, London School of Economics, no. 31 (September 1991); A.K. Sen, "Equality of What?" in S. Murrin, ed., *Tanner Lectures on Human Values*, vol. 1 (Cambridge: Cambridge University Press, 1980); and A.K. Sen, "Rights as Goals," in S. Guest and A. Milne, eds., *Equality and Discrimination: Essays in Freedom and Justice* (Stuttgart: Franz Steiner, 1985).

2. Quoted in Doris Kearns Goddwin, *No Ordinary Time: Franklin and Eleanor Roosevelt. The Home Front in World War II* (New York: Simon & Schuster, 1994), p. 485.

3. Vaclav Havel, "Foreword," in N. Barr, ed., *Labor Markets and Social Policy in Central and Eastern Europe: The Transition and Beyond* (London: Oxford University Press, 1994).

4. Albert Hirschman, *Exit, Voice, and Loyalty: Responses to Decline in Firms, Organizations, and States* (Cambridge, MA: Harvard University Press, 1970).

5. The Russian transition has been greatly influenced by the rise of free market ideology in the West, and the collapse of communism has contributed to growing sentiments against government regulation and welfare-state policies. For a critical discussion of the limits of free market theory and ideology for the Russian transition, see J.E. Stiglitz, *Whither Socialism?* (Cambridge, MA: MIT Press, 1994); A.H. Amsden, J. Kochanowicz, and L. Taylor, *The Market Meets Its Match* (Cambridge, MA: Harvard University Press, 1994); and B. Silverman, R. Vogt, and M. Yanowitch, eds., *Labor and Democracy in the Transition to a Market System* (Armonk, NY: M.E. Sharpe, 1992).

6. Anders Aslund, *How Russia Became a Market Economy* (Washington, DC: Brookings Institution, 1995), p. 88.

7. Karl Polanyi, *The Great Transformation: The Political and Economic Organization of Our Time* (Boston: Beacon Press, 1960).

8. *Ekonomicheskie i sotsial'nye peremeny: Monitoring obshchestvennogo mneniia*, 1994, no. 2, p. 74.

9. Tat'iana Zaslavskaia, *The Second Socialist Revolution* (Bloomington and Indianapolis: Indiana University Press, 1990).

10. For an excellent discussion of the ideological dimensions of the transition and their limitations, see Moshe Lewin, *Russia/USSR/Russia: The Drive and Drift of a Super State* (New York: The New Press, 1995), pp. 306–330.

11. R.V. Daniels, "Russia's Road to Oz: Utopian Reforms vs. Modern Reality," *Dissent*, Summer 1995, p. 308.

12. P. Murrell, "The Transition According to Cambridge, Mass.," *Journal of Economic Literature*, March 1995, pp. 164–178.

13. For a strong defense of radical economic reform, see Aslund, *How Russia Became a Market Economy*. An alternative perspective can be found in Amsden et al., *The Market Meets Its Match*; and M. Goldman, *Lost Opportunities: Why Economic Reforms in Russia Have Not Worked* (New York: W.W. Norton, 1994); P. Desai, "Shock Therapy and Russia: Was It Tried? Why Did It Fail? What Did It Do?" Discussion Paper no. 692, Columbia University Economics Department, May 1994.

14. *The Current Digest of the Post-Soviet Press*, vol. 47 (1995), no. 10, pp. 7–8.

15. Lewin, *Russia/USSR/Russia*, pp. 318–319.

16. Aslund, *How Russia Became a Market Economy*, p. 87.

17. One illustration reveals the ideological dimension of the debate. In answering some of the critics of radical reform, a member of the Gaidar team responded in the following manner:

> It is typical that any critic of the Russian reform program . . . invariably cites the same person, naming someone who is an opponent of the entire world community of economists: Galbraith. . . . They have no other authorities . . . and for Russian readers in contrast to Westerners, he is a big name—as a consequence of his leftist political positions, Galbraith was perhaps the only American economist who was translated and commented on approvingly in the official political economy course. . . . But Galbraith never dealt with problems of macroeconomic stabilization.

See *The Current Digest of the Post-Soviet Press,* vol. 44, no. 12 (1992), p. 4. The reader should note that Galbraith was director of the Office of Price Stabilization during World War II.

18. A.O. Hirschman, *Rival Views of Market Society* (Cambridge, MA: Harvard University Press, 1992), p. vi.

19. A.M. Okun, *Equality and Efficiency: The Big Trade-Off* (Washington, DC: Brookings Institution, 1975).

20. See, for example, Robert Barro, "Economic Growth in a Cross Section of Countries," *Quarterly Journal of Economics*, vol. 106 (1991), no. 2, pp. 407–443; Nancy Stokey, "Human Capital, Product Quality and Growth," *Quarterly Journal of Economics*, vol. 106 (1991), no. 2, pp. 587–616; and other articles in this issue; see also Sylvia Nasar, "Economics of Equality: A New View," *New York Times*, January 9, 1994, pp. 9 and 48, as well as the works of Nancy Birdall, Richard Sabor, Alberto Alesina, and Roberto Perotti.

21. Quoted in B. Silverman, R. Vogt, and M. Yanowitch, eds., *Double Shift: Transforming Work in Postsocialist and Postindustrial Societies* (Armonk, NY: M.E. Sharpe, 1993), p. xxiv.

22. Many textbooks, including Samuelson's, argued that authoritarian planning might be a superior way of inducing economic growth. See Stiglitz, *Whither Socialism?* p. 4.

23. A.B. Atkinson, and J. Mickelwright, *Economic Transformation in Eastern Europe and the Distribution of Income* (New York: Cambridge University Press, 1992).

24. Robert M. Solow, *The Labor Market as a Social Institution* (Cambridge, MA: Basil Blackwell, 1990), pp. 23–24.

25. Stiglitz, *Whither Socialism?* pp. 49–50; 265–66.

26. Chrystia Freeland, "Capitalism Exposes the Poverty Gap," *Financial Times*, April 10, 1995, pp. 1–2.

Notes to Chapter 2

1. "Once More on the Results of Shock Therapy," *Nezavisimaia gazeta*, February 3, 1994, pp. 1, 4. This is a portion of a report prepared by the Economics Division of the Russian Academy of Sciences and the International Reform Foundation. Comments on this report in the Russian press imply that Shatalin, Abalkin, and Petrakov participated in its preparation (see, for example, *Izvestiia*, January 29, 1994, pp. 1–2). Some of the other critical literature we draw on in this section include the following: Stanislav Shatalin, "The Market Requires Management," *Ekonomika i zhizn'*, February 1994, no. 5, p. 1; Institute of Economics, "The Social and Economic Situation in Russia: Results, Problems, Paths of Stabilization," *Voprosy ekonomiki*, 1994, no. 2, pp. 126–160; Oleg Bogomolov, "Reforms After Gaidar," *Nezavisimaia gazeta*, February 8, 1994, p. 2.

2. "Once More on the Results of Shock Therapy."

3. Shatalin, "The Market Requires Management."

4. "Once More on the Results of Shock Therapy."

5. *Russian Economic Trends*, vol. 5, no. 2, pp. 77–78. For an argument that output declines have been inflated see Anders Aslund, *How Russia Became a Market Economy* (Washington, DC: The Brookings Institution, 1995), p. 278.

6. For a higher estimate of the proportion of the population below the poverty level, see Tat'iana Zaslavskaia, "The Incomes of the Working Population of Russia," *Ekonomicheskie i sotsial'nye peremeny: Monitoring obshchestvennogo mneniia*, 1994, no. 1, pp. 5–10. For somewhat lower estimates of the extent of impoverishment than shown in Table 2.2, see Gosudarstvennyi komitet Rossiiskoi Federatsii po statistike, *Sotsial'no-ekonomicheskoe polozhenie Rossiiskoi Federatsii v ianvare-noiabre 1993 goda* (Moscow, 1993), p. 64. The official data on poverty are presented in Table 3.2.

7. "Once More on the Results of Shock Therapy."

8. *Sotsial'no-ekonomicheskoe polozhenie Rossiiskoi Federatsii v ianvare-noiabre 1993 goda*, pp. 72–73; Andrei Baiduzhii, "A Demographic Catastrophe Has Become a Reality," *Nezavisimaia gazeta*, February 2, 1994, p. 1.

9. *Russian Economic Trends*, vol. 4, no. 4, pp. 49, 53.

10. Vladimir Mikhalev, "Poverty Alleviation in the Course of Transition: Policy Options for Russia," unpublished paper presented to Robert Schuman Centre, European University, Florence, Italy (June 1996), p. 6.

11. *Russian Economic Trends*, vol. 4, no. 4, p. 65.

12. Ibid.

13. Goskomstat, *Informatsionnyi statisticheskii biulleten'*, no. 13 (Moscow, 1995), pp. 28–29.

14. Cited in Michael Kramer, "Russia '96," *Time*, May 27, 1996, p. 56.

15. Centre for Co-operation with the Economies in Transition, *OECD Economic Surveys: The Russian Federation* (Paris, 1995), p. 121.

16. Amartya Sen, "Beyond Liberalization: Social Opportunities and Human Capability," Development Economics Research Program, London School of Economics, no. 58 (November 1994), p. 32.

17. *Russian Economic Trends*, vol. 4, no. 1, p. 64.

18. Mikhalev, "Poverty Alleviation," p. 14.

19. *OECD Economic Surveys*, p. 124.

20. Ibid., p. 126.

21. *Russian Economic Trends*, vol. 5, no. 2, p. 105.

22. See, for example, the work of Judith Shapiro cited in Aslund, *How Russia Became a Market Economy*, pp. 287–88.

23. Mikhalev, "Poverty Alleviation," p. 7.

24. Tat'iana Zaslavskaia, *The Second Socialist Revolution* (Bloomington and Indianapolis: Indiana University Press, 1990), p. 131.

25. Gennadii Lisichkin, "A Prosperous Worker—A Thriving State," *Izvestiia*, August 8, 1989.

26. Natal'ia Rimashevskaia, "On the Methodology of Defining the Qualitative Conditions of the Population," in N.M. Rimashevskaia and V.G. Kopnina, eds., *Kachestvo naseleniia* (Moscow, 1993), p. 17.

27. Shatalin, "The Market Requires Management." See also the Institute of Economics, "The Social and Economic Situation in Russia," p. 134, which treats increasing income differentials as evidence of the "acuteness of social problems."

28. Natal'ia Rimashevskaia, "The Rich and the Poor," *Trud*, January 18, 1994, p. 5.

29. Iurii Sukhotin, "Stabilization of the Economy and Social Contrasts," *Svobodnaia mysl'*, 1994, no. 1, p. 23.

30. Egor Gaidar, "The Most Correct Policy Is a Responsible Policy, Not Populism," *EKO*, 1993, no. 11, pp. 5–6.

31. Ibid., pp. 6–8.

32. See, for example, Shatalin, "The Market Requires Management."

33. Nina Naumova, "Social Policy Under Conditions of Delayed Modernization," *Sotsiologicheskii zhurnal*, no. 1, 1994, pp. 6–21.

34. Sukhotin, "Stabilization of the Economy and Social Contrasts."

35. Rimashevskaia, "The Rich and the Poor."

36. For an assertion that this was, in fact, the case, see G.I. Khanin, "The End of Illusions," *EKO*, 1992, no. 10, p. 32.

37. Z. Golenkova, ed., *Sotsial'naia struktura i stratifikatsiia grazhdanskogo obshchestva v Rossii* (Moscow: Institute of Sociology, 1995), p. 7.

38. Larisa Zubova, "Material Position, Personal Incomes, and Savings: Estimates and Tendencies," *Ekonomicheskie i sotsial'nye peremeny: Monitoring obshchestvennogo mneniia*, 1994, no. 3, p. 27.

39. L.A. Khakhulina, "The Attitude of the Population to the Differentiation of

Incomes and Social Stratification," *Ekonomicheskie i sotsial'nye peremeny: Monitoring obshchestvennogo mneniia*, 1993, no. 4, p. 7.

40. Ibid., pp. 8–9.

41. Brigitte Granville, Judith Shapiro, and Oksanna Dynnikova, "Less Inflation, Less Poverty: First Results for Russia," unpublished paper, April 8, 1996.

42. Brigitte Granville, *The Success of Russian Economic Reforms* (Great Britain: The Royal Institute of International Affairs, 1996).

43. *The Current Digest of the Post-Soviet Press*, vol. 54 (1992), no. 45, p. 10.

44. Amartya Sen, "Beyond Liberalization: Social Opportunity and Human Capability," The Development Economics Research Programme, London School of Economics, no. 58 (November 1994), p. 5.

45. Ibid., p. 32.

46. Michael Specter, "Grim Yeltsin Blames His Government for Russia's Ills," *Financial Times*, February 24, 1996, p. 1.

47. Thomas Friedman, "14 Big Macs Later . . . " *New York Times*, December 31, 1995, Section 4, p. 9.

Notes to Chapter 3

1. Alastair McAuley, *Economic Welfare in the Soviet Union* (Madison: University of Wisconsin Press, 1979), p. 357.

2. Anthony Atkinson and John Micklewright, *Economic Transformation in Eastern Europe and the Distribution of Income* (Cambridge: Cambridge University Press, 1992), p. 191.

3. Tat'iana Iarygina, "Poverty in Rich Russia," *Obshchestvennye nauki i sovremennost'*, 1994, no. 2, pp. 27–28; Atkinson and Micklewright, *Economic Transformation in Eastern Europe*, p. 192.

4. McAuley, *Economic Welfare in the Soviet Union*, p. 70.

5. See, for example, G. Valiuzhenich, "The Rich and the Poor," *Argumenty i fakty*, 1990, no. 45, p. 1; "The Subsistence Minimum: For Whom and for What Is It Needed," *Sotsialisticheskii trud*, 1991, no. 9, p. 25; L. Zubova, et al., "Poverty in the USSR," *Problems of Economics*, vol. 34, no. 10 (February 1992), p. 86.

6. For an excellent recent analysis of poverty issues, see Vladimir Mikhalev, "Poverty Alleviation in the Course of Transition: Policy Options for Russia," unpublished working paper, Robert Schuman Centre, European University Institute, Florence, Italy (June 1996), p. 6.

7. A. Kovalev, "Who Is Below the Poverty Line and Why?" *Argumenty i fakty*, 1989, no. 25, p. 11; Institut sotsial'no-ekonomicheskikh problem narodonaseleniia, *Perestroika v sisteme raspredelitel'nykh otnoshenii* (Moscow, 1992), pp. 81–86.

8. Atkinson and Micklewright, *Economic Transformation in Eastern Europe*, p. 241.

9. Natal'ia Rimashevskaia, "Our Subsistence Minimum," *Sotsialisticheskii trud*, 1990, no. 8, p. 68; A. Kovalev, "Who Is Below the Poverty Line and Why?" p. 11; Institut sotsial'no-ekonomicheskikh problem narodonaseleniia, *Ekonomicheskie reformy v Rossii: Sotsial'noe izmerenie*, no. 8 (Moscow, 1993), p. 34.

10. G. Valiuzhenich, for example, cites 78 rubles per month as the subsistence minimum reported by "the government," 90 rubles as the figure accepted by the State Committee on Labor of the USSR, and "about 130 rubles" as the figure set by the trade union. See Valiuzhenich, "The Rich and the Poor."

11. We rely here on Boris Rakitskii's citation of Yeltsin's remarks in "The Condition of the Population of Russia," *Problems of Economic Transition*, vol. 36, no. 10 (February 1994), p. 33. Yeltsin's remarks apparently appeared originally in *Rossiiskaia gazeta*, October 29, 1991.

12. Alexander Samorodov, "Transition, Poverty and Inequality in Russia," *International Labor Review*, vol. 131 (1992), no. 3, p. 340.

13. Marina Mozhina, "The Poor: What is the Boundary Line," *Problems of Economic Transition*, vol. 35, (October 1992) no. 6, p. 69.

14. Atkinson and Micklewright, *Economic Transformation in Eastern Europe*, p. 185.

15. Mozhina, "The Poor," pp. 27–32.

16. Centre for Co-operation with Economies in Transition, *OECD Economic Surveys: The Russian Federation* (Paris, 1995), p. 124.

17. Mikhalev, "Poverty Alleviation," p. 9.

18. G. Valiuzhenich, "The Survival Threshold," *Argumenty i fakty*, 1993, no. 4, p. 3.

19. Compare the material in ibid., and in *Rossiiskie vesti*, April 21, 1994, p. 1.

20. Valiuzhenich, "The Survival Threshold."

21. Excerpts from a report of the Institute of Economic Problems of the Transition Period, "Monetary-Credit and Budget Policy in Russia in 1993," *Obshchestvo i ekonomika*, 1994, no. 5–6, p. 111.

22. Larissa Zubova, Natal'ia Kovaleva, and Ludmila Khakhulina, "Poverty Under New Economic Conditions," *Ekonomicheskie i sotsial'nye peremeny: Monitoring obshchestvennogo mneniia*, 1994, no. 4, p. 25.

23. *Russian Economic Trends, Monthly Update*, June 30, 1994, p. 43. This source shows 72 percent of families with three or more children and 55 percent of single-parent families as below the poverty level during July–September 1992. Viacheslav Bobkov, "The Russian Population's Living Standard During the Reform Period," *Svobodnaia mysl'*, 1993, no. 16, p. 30, indicates that "up to 60 percent" of these groups could be classified as "poor" in mid-1993.

24. Russian Economic Trends, Monthly Update, June 30, 1994, p. 43, shows 46 percent of children up to the age of six and 47 percent of children ages seven to fifteen as living below the poverty level during July–September 1992. Goskomstat Rossii, Sotsial'no-ekonomicheskoe polozhenie Rossiiskoi Federatsii v ianvare-noiabre 1993 goda (Moscow, 1993), p. 65, shows 38.7 percent of children to age six and 39.6 percent of children aged seven to fifteen as living in poverty in 1993.

25. Vladimir Mikhalev, "Social Security in Russia Under Economic Transformation," *Europe-Asia Studies*, vol. 48 (1996), no. 1, p. 15.

26. Mikhalev, "Social Security in Russia," p. 20.

27. Unfortunately, the authors of this study do not explain why unskilled workers represented a surprisingly small proportion of the working poor (11 percent), and do not clarify which particular occupational groups were included in

the "skilled workers" classification that accounted for fully 50 percent of the main breadwinners in families of the working poor.

28. The only exception is that the money income of peasants is lower than that of unskilled workers, while their real income is higher.

29. Tat'iana Zaslavskaia, "Real Incomes of Russians Through the Prism of Social Assessments," *Obshchestvo i ekonomika*, 1994, no. 3–4, p. 73.

30. Ibid., p. 70.

31. The other side of these differences in poverty rates is reflected in the very different proportions of wage-earners and "owners of enterprises" classified at the upper end of Zaslavskaia's scale of economic gradations, that is, as "well-to-do" or "prosperous." Only 8 percent of wage-earners fell into these classifications, but 65 percent of "owners of enterprises" did so. Ibid., pp. 69–70.

32. Ibid., p. 73.

33. Richard W. Stevenson, "Did Yeltsin Get a Sweetheart Deal on IMF Loans?" *New York Times*, March 11, 1996, p. 11.

34. Branko Milanovic, *Poverty, Inequality and Social Policy in Transition Economies* (Washington, DC: World Bank, 1995), p.3.

35. UNICEF, *Poverty, Children and Policy for a Brighter Future* (Florence, Italy: International Child Development Centre, 1995).

36. Rachel L. Swarns, "Moscow Sends Homeless to Far Away Hometowns," *New York Times*, October 15, 1996, pp. 1, 12.

37. Goskomstat Rossii, *Uroven' zhizni naseleniia Rossii* (Moscow, 1996), p. 86.

Notes to Chapter 4

1. Gail Warshofsky Lapidus, *Women in Soviet Society* (Berkeley: University of California Press, 1978); Murray Yanowitch, *Social and Economic Inequality in the Soviet Union* (White Plains, NY: M.E. Sharpe, 1977), ch. 6.

2. Institute of Economics, *Rabotaiushchie zhenshchiny u usloviiakh perekhoda Rossii k rynku* (Moscow, 1993), p. 4.

3. Monica S. Fong, *The Role of Women in Rebuilding the Russian Economy*, Studies of Economies in Transformation, Paper No. 10 (Washington, DC: World Bank, 1993), p. 14.

4. Murray Yanowitch, *Social and Economic Inequality*, pp. 172–174.

5. In practice, these restrictions on women's work were frequently ignored or violated. Natal'ia Rimashevskia, "Social Policy and Labor Legislation," in B. Silverman, R. Vogt, and M. Yanowitch, eds., *Double Shift: Transforming Work in Postsocialist and Postindustrial Societies* (Armonk, NY: M.E. Sharpe, 1993), p. 88.

6. Ulla Wikander, Alice Kessler-Harris, and Jane Lewis, eds., *Protecting Women: Labor Legislation in Europe, the United States, and Australia, 1880–1920* (Urbana: University of Illinois Press, 1995), p. 1.

7. Mikhail Gorbachev, *Perestroika: New Thinking for Our Country and the World* (New York: Harper & Row, 1987), p. 117.

8. Ibid.

9. Earnings in at least one sector with a large proportion of women employees—credit and state insurance—increased at a more rapid rate than average earnings in the economy as a whole.

10. Tat'iana Boldyreva, "You Won't Stop the Revolutionary Horse in His Tracks," *EKO*, 1988, no. 8, p. 142.

11. Liudmila Rzhanitsyna, "The Work Is Not Always Good, But Necessary," *Chelovek i trud*, 1993, nos. 5–6, p. 15.

12. Institut sotsial'no-ekonomicheskikh problem narodonaseleniia (henceforth ISEPN), *Sem'ia i semeinaia politika* (Moscow, 1991), p. 54.

13. Gail Warshofsky Lapidus, "Gender and Restructuring: The Impact of Perestroika and its Aftermath on Soviet Women," in V.M. Moghadam, ed., *Democratic Reform and the Position of Women in Transitional Economies* (Oxford: Clarendon Press, 1993), p. 153.

14. Boldyreva, "You Won't Stop the Revolutionary Horse," pp. 148–149.

15. Ibid., p. 149.

16. We rely here on the following: Natal'ia Zakharova, Anastasia Posodskaia, and Natal'ia Rimashevskaia, "How We Are Resolving the Women Question," *Kommunist*, 1989, no. 4, pp. 56–65; ISEPN, *Sem'ia i semeinaia politika*, pp. 47–57; ISEPN, *Zhenshchina i sotsial'naia politika* (Moscow, 1992), pp. 6–9.

17. ISEPN, *Sem'ia i semeinaia politika*, p. 47.

18. Ibid.

19. Boldyreva, "You Won't Stop the Revolutionary Horse," p. 148.

20. Institute of Economics, *Rabotaiushchie zhenshchiny*, p. 5.

21. It should be recalled that the various categories of economic status used by Zaslavskaia are based on public perceptions of a "minimum subsistence" income, "normal" income, and (for the upper gradations of economic status) multiples of "normal" income.

22. Even economists critical of the feminist perspective on gender inequality came to similar conclusions. A study conducted in April 1994 by the Center for Labor Market Studies, based on a survey of 1,088 women in Ivanovo and Nizhnii Novgorod, found that 80.7 percent of the women surveyed received wages below the national average of 171,500 rubles. Thirty-four percent received wages of less than 50,000 rubles per month at a time when the subsistence minimum wage was estimated at 74,800 rubles. Another 38.5 percent earned between 50,000 to 100,000 rubles.

A survey of company managers conducted in January 1995 also confirmed women's limited success among this more privileged group. More than two-thirds (67.9 percent) of female managers earned 400,000 rubles or less per month, while slightly more than two-thirds (66.8 percent) of the male managers earned 400,000 rubles or more per month. Male managers were almost three times as likely as women to be in this higher income group. Average family per capita income of male and female managers reveals a similar pattern, dispelling the view that most female managers were simply adding income to an already privileged household. See Institute of Economics, Center for Labor Market Studies, *The Position of Women in a Reformed Economy: The Russian Experience* (Moscow, 1995), p. 39.

23. The literature of this period constantly refers to gender asymmetry. ISEPN, *Zhenshchina i sotsial'naia politika*, p. 7; ISEPN, *Ekonomicheskie reformy v Rossii: Sotsial'noe izmerenie* (Moscow, 1993), p. 126.

24. Sergei Iu. Roshchin, "Special Features of Women's Employment in the Transitional Economy of Russia," Candidate of Economic Science dissertation presented to Economics Faculty, Moscow State University (Moscow, 1995), p. 10. The author uses an index of occupational segregation, the "Duncan index," which shows a steady rise in segmentation from 1940 through 1993. See also Andrew Newell and Barry Reilly, "The Gender Wage Gap in Russia," presented at Seminar on Gender in Transition, Bucharest, Romania, February 1–2, 1995. The authors conclude that occupation segregation in Russia is more severe than in other Western countries.

25. Calculated from earnings figures in Goskomstat Rossii, *Rossiiskaia Federatsiia v tsifrakh v 1992 godu* (Moscow, 1993), pp. 70–71.

26. *Kommersant-Daily*, November 21, 1995.

27. Calculated from data in Institute of Economics, Center for Labor Market Studies, *The Position of Women in a Reformed Economy*, pp. 41–42.

28. Fong, *The Role of Women*, pp. 3, 17.

29. Goskomstat Rossii, *Uroven' zhizni naseleniia Rossii*, Moscow, 1996, pp. 180, 184.

30. *Russian Economic Trends*, vol. 4 (1995), no. 1, p. 53.

31. The following data on employment are derived from the State Committee of the Russian Federation, *Information Statistical Bulletin*, no. 9 (August 1995).

32. Sergei Roshchin, "Discrimination and Equality of Opportunity on the Labor Market," *Chelovek i trud*, 1995, no. 4, pp. 14–16.

33. The material in this paragraph draws on the following: ISEPN, *Zhenshchina i sotsial'naia politika*, pp. 8, 25, 47; ISEPN, *Ekonomicheskie reformy v Rossii*, pp. 127, 131; ISEPN, *Deti Rossii: Sotsial'no-ekonomisheskie problemy* (Moscow, 1994), pp. 40–42.

34. Ibid., p. 72.

35. Ibid., p. 89. However, the advocates of this position made it clear that they had in mind a "civilized labor market."

36. Institute of Economics, Center for Labor Market Studies, *The Position of Women in a Reformed Economy: The Russian Experience*, p. 16.

37. Ibid., p. 5.

38. Ibid.

39. Ibid.

40. Ibid., p. 6.

41. Roshchin, "Special Features of Women's Employment," p. 11.

42. "The Conception of Social Policy in Russia (From a Report to the Institute of Socioeconomic Problems of the Population)," *Obshchestvennye nauki i sovremennost'*, 1994, no. 6, pp. 29–30.

43. N.S. Iulina, "Women, the Family, and Society: Discussions in the Feminist Thought of the United States," *Voprosy filosofii*, 1994, no. 9, pp. 145–146; English translation in *Russian Studies in Philosophy,* vol. 34, no.2 (Fall 1995), pp.73–96.

Notes to Chapter 5

1. Tat'iana Zaslavskaia, *The Second Socialist Revolution* (Bloomington and Indianapolis: Indiana University Press, 1990), p. 62.

Work in Postsocialist and Postindustrial Societies (Armonk, NY: M.E. Sharpe, 1992), p. 22.

3. See Vladimir Gimpelson, "Economic Consciousness and Reform of the Employment Sphere," in ibid., pp. 39–52.

4. Iurii Volkov, "The Market Economy and Ensuring Social Justice in the Sphere of Labor Relations," *Problems of Economic Transition*, vol. 35, (September 1992), no. 5, pp. 50–56.

5. Tat'iana Zaslavskaia, "The Individual in Russian Society in the Midst of Reform," *Obshchestvo i ekonomika*, 1995, no. 9, p. 3.

6. Ibid., p. 3.

7. Ibid., p. 8.

8. Leonid Gordon, "Poverty in Contemporary Russian Society," in L.A. Beliaeva, ed., *Sotsial'naia stratifikatsiia sovremennogo russiiskogo obshchestvo* (Moscow, 1995), p. 61.

9. Institute of Sociology, Russian Academy of Sciences, *Sotsial'naia struktura i stratifikatsiia v usloviiakh formirovaniia grazhdanskogo obshchestvo v Rossii* (Moscow, 1995), p. 7.

10. Institute of Socioeconomic Problems of the Population, Laboratory of Distributive Relations, "Permissible Limits of Differentiation of Incomes in Society," unpublished paper (Moscow, 1994), p. 17.

11. Ekaterina Khibovskaia, "The Dynamic of Incomes," *Ekonomicheskie i sotsial'nye peremeny: Monitoring obshchestvennogo mneniia*, 1994, no. 6, p. 37.

12. Gordon, "Poverty in Contemporary Russian Society," p. 50.

13. OECD, *Wage Formation During the Period of Economic Restructuring in the Russian Federation* (Paris, 1995), p. 40.

14. The relative earnings of medical personnel remained essentially constant at three-quarters of the average for the economy as a whole between 1991 and 1994.

15. Ibid. See also Alastair McAuley, *Social Welfare in Transition: What Happened in Russia* (Washington, DC: World Bank, 1994).

16. This section draws largely on Tat'iana Zaslavskaia, "The Structure of Today's Russian Society," *Ekonomicheskie i sotsial'nye peremeny: Monitoring obshchestvennogo mneniia*, 1995, no. 6, pp. 11–13. Zaslavskaia also identifies an "upper-level intelligentsia" stratum distinct from the mass intelligentsia, and a "workers' elite" distinct from the industrial workers' stratum. A substantial majority of these two highly skilled (or highly placed) groups live in "relative comfort" and have earnings well above those of the mass intelligentsia and industrial workers. Numerically, however, they are considerably less important than the latter two groups.

17. OECD, *Wage Formation*, p. 23.

18. "A striking development of the transition is that professionals and engineers who had traditionally been underpaid in Russia have lost more ground in recent years." Ibid., p. 22. A VTsIOM study conducted in mid-1994 showed that the wages of "specialists" (a category that seemed to include the bulk of engineering-technical personnel) were actually slightly below the earnings of skilled urban workers (Khibovskaia, "The Dynamic of Incomes," p. 34).

19. Institute of Socioeconomic Problems of the Population, Laboratory of Distributive Relations, "Permissible Limits of Differentiation of Incomes in Society," p. 20.

20. Ministry of Labor of the Russian Federation, "On the Results of Socioeco-

nomic Development of the Russian Federation in the First Six Months of 1994 and Tasks for the Immediate Future," *Profsoiuznoe obozrenie*, 1994, no. 7, p. 30.

21. Khibovskaia, "The Dynamic of Incomes," pp. 33–34. Other studies that accept the notion that an increasing relative wage advantage for top managerial personnel accompanied the marketizing reforms of the early post-Soviet period include OECD, *Wage Formation*, p. 23, and Institute of Socioeconomic Problems of the Population, Laboratory of Distributive Relations, "Permissible Limits of Differentiation of Incomes in Society," p. 20.

22. Vladimir Gimpelson, "Employment Patterns in Russia, Private Sector Developments: Employment and Wages," unpublished paper presented to Center for the Study of Labor and Democracy, Hofstra University, 1996.

23. The employment figures on which we rely here apply mainly to the state and the former state sector (privatized former state enterprises). Apparently they do not cover part of the "new" private sector created apart from the privatization of former state firms. See *Russian Economic Trends*, vol. 4, no. 4, p. 92.

24. V. Kosmarskii and T. Maleva, "Social Policy in Russia in the Context of Macroeconomic Reform," *Voprosy ekonomiki*, 1995, no. 9, p. 10.

25. A study by L.A. Khakhulina does not reveal marked changes in people's fear of losing their jobs within the 1992–95 period. But it does show that the fear of job loss was much greater throughout this period than it was in 1989. L.A. Khakhulina, "Workers' Behavior on the Labor Market Under Conditions of a Transition to a Market Economy," paper Presented at a Conference on "Social Policy Under Conditions of Financial Stabilization: New Solutions to Old Problems," Moscow, April 1996, Table 1.

26. Among the factors cited by Vladimir Gimpelson to explain the relatively small proportion of jobless registered with the Federal Employment Service (FES) are the following: the extremely low level of unemployment benefits, "lack of trust in government institutions, widespread belief that the FES has no vacancies that could fit a jobseeker's need, bad outreach of parts of the population by FES offices." See Vladimir Gimpelson, "Is Employment in Russia Restructured?" paper presented at NATO Economic Colloquium, June 26–28, 1996, p. 2

27. Khakhulina, "Workers' Behavior on the Labor Market," p. 2.

28. Gimpelson, "Is Employment in Russia Restructured?" p. 3.

29. Z.T. Golenkova, "The Transformation of the Social Structure of Russian Society," *Obshchestvo i ekonomika*, 1995, no. 9, p. 14.

30. Khakhulina, "Workers' Behavior on the Labor Market," p. 2.

31. The VTsIOM study, which estimated that 10 percent of the working-age population did not have jobs but was seeking employment at the end of 1995, also found the following: 40 percent of those without work had voluntarily left their last job; 35 percent had lost their last job because of plant closings or reductions in staff; and 15 percent were unable to find work after completing school. Khakhulina, "Workers' Behavior on the Labor Market," p. 2. However, the source on which we rely here also notes that there was a significant decline in the relative magnitude of voluntary quits between 1993 and 1995, and an increase in the role of the other two factors cited above.

32. Kosmarskii and Maleva, "Social Policy in Russia," p. 6; Center for Cooperation with the Economies in Transition, *OECD Economic Surveys: The Russian Federation* (Paris, 1995), p. 113.

33. *Russian Economic Trends*, vol. 5 (1996), no. 2, p. 54.

34. Center for Cooperation with the Economies in Transition, OECD, *The Russian Federation*, pp. 111–112.

35. Kosmarskii and Maleva, "Social Policy in Russia," p. 9.

36. Ibid., p. 15.

37. A study conducted late in 1994 (unlike the study whose findings are shown in Table 5.10) whose published findings are confined to "registered" unemployed women in a single district in Moscow identified 58 percent of the unemployed women as specialists and only 24.5 percent as workers. But the source available to us says nothing about the occupational composition of unemployed men in this district. The fact that this study was confined to a single region of Moscow makes it of limited value for our purposes, but it does imply that at least in some areas a substantial proportion of the unemployed were people with relatively high levels of education. See E.B. Gruzdeva, *Zhenskaia bezrabotitsa v Rossii (1991–1994 gg.)* (Moscow, 1995), pp. 30–32.

38. K. Khagemayer, A. Nesporova, and D. Von Whitehead, "The Role of Policy in Education, the Labor Market, Wages, and the Social Sphere in Stimulating Employment in Russia," *Obshchestvo i ekonomika*, 1996, no. 3–4, p. 103.

Notes to Chapter 6

1. Eric Hobsbawm, *The Age of Extremes: A History of the World, 1914–1991* (New York: Pantheon Books, 1994), p. 472.

2. For a review of this subject see Maxim Boycko, A. Shleifer, and R. Vishny, *Privatizing Russia* (Cambridge, MA: The MIT Press, 1995); Roman Frydman, A. Rapaczynski, and J. Earle, *The Privatization Process in Russia, Ukraine and the Baltic States* (Budapest: Central European Press, 1993); and Lynn D. Nelson and I. Kuzes, *Property to the People: The Struggle for Radical Economic Reform in Russia* (Armonk, NY: M.E. Sharpe, 1994).

3. Boycko et al., *Privatizing Russia*, p. 48.

4. Tat'iana Zaslavskaia, "The Business Stratum of Russian Society: Essence, Structure, and Status," *Obshchestvennye nauki i sovremennost'*, 1995, no. 1, p. 18.

5. Evgenii Starikov, "Russian Society After One Perestroika and Two Putsches," *Znanie-sila*, 1994, no. 8, p. 6.

6. Ibid., p. 8.

7. Viacheslav Smol'kov, "Entrepreneurship as a Special Type of Activity," *Sotsiologicheskie issledovaniia*, 1994, no. 2, p. 15.

8. Ibid., p. 16.

9. Ibid., p. 21.

10. Leonid Gordon, "Russian Society After One Perestroika and Two Putsches," *Znanie–sila*, 1994, no. 10, p. 63.

11. Egor Gaidar, *Gosudarstvo i evoliutsiia* (Moscow, 1995), p. 195.

12. Ibid., pp. 165–166.

13. Chrystia Freeland, John Thornhill, and Andrew Gowers, "Moscow's Group of Seven," *Financial Times*, November 1, 1996, p. 15.

14. Ibid.

15. *Ekonomicheskie i sotsial'nye peremeny: Monitoring obshchestvennogo mneniia*, 1993, no. 4, p. 53.

16. Tat′iana Zaslavskaia, "The Business Stratum of Russian Society: Essence, Structure and Status," *Sotsiologicheskie issledovaniia*, 1995, no. 3, p. 9.

17. Actually, Zaslavskaia notes that the average reported incomes of the businessmen included in her study were some two and a half to three times the incomes of wage-earners ("hired working people"). If we exclude from the business stratum one group that Zaslavskaia includes in it—salaried managers not engaged in private business and wholly dependent on wage income—the differential between business and wage income (in favor of the former) is threefold or higher. Zaslavskaia herself expressed some doubt as to the legitimacy of including the above group of salaried managers in the business stratum. See Zaslavskaia, "The Business Stratum of Russian Society," pp. 30, 32.

18. Ibid., p. 32.

19. Ia. Roshchina, *Stil′ zhizny Moskovskikh predprinimatelei: Empiricheskie tipologii iz struktury pozitsii* (Moscow, 1995), p. 8.

20. This section draws mainly on the following sources: Vladimir Gimpelson, "New Russian Entrepreneurship: Sources of Formation and Strategy of Social Action," *Mirovaia ekonomika i mezhdunarodnye otnosheniia*, 1993, no. 6, pp. 31–42; O. Perepelkin, "The Russian Entrepreneur: Features of a Social Portrait," *Sotsiologicheskie issledovanii*, 1995, no. 2, pp. 35–40; V. Radaev, "New Russian Entrepreneurship in the Judgment of Experts," *Mir Rossii*, 1994, no. 1, pp. 36–54; V. Radaev, "Russian Entrepreneurs—Who Are They?" *Vestnik statistiki*, 1993, no. 9, pp. 3–13; Zhanna Grishchenko, Lidiia Novikova, and Igor Lapsha, "A Social Portrait of the Entrepreneur (Minsk, Spring 1992)," *Sotsiologicheskie issledovaniia*, 1992, no. 10, pp. 53–61; Iurii Popov, "Russian Entrepreneurship: A Social Portrait," *Chelovek i trud*, 1995, no. 2, pp. 92–97.

21. Gimpelson, "New Russian Entrepreneurship," p. 36.

22. Perepelkin, "The Russian Entrepreneur," p. 39.

23. Popov, "Russian Entrepreneurship," p. 95.

24. Gimpelson, "New Russian Entrepreneurship," p. 35.

25. Additional evidence of the minor role of workers as sources of recruitment into business activity appears in Grishchenko et al., "A Social Portrait of the Entrepreneur," p. 53. It is possible, of course, that some of the directors and other managerial personnel that moved into private business operations began their work careers in workers' or peasants' jobs. But if they did, their movement into managerial and other higher-level positions probably reflects social mobility in the Soviet period.

26. For an expression of this view, see I.M. Bunin, "A Social Portrait of the Small and Medium-Sized Business in Russia," *Politicheskie issledovaniia*, 1993, no. 3, pp. 149–154.

27. Perepelkin, "The Russian Entrepreneur," p. 40. Although the author refers here mainly to the sectors that "young entrepreneurs" tended to enter, other sources make it clear that the general economic environment made these sectors attractive to new business operators generally.

28. Radaev, "Russian Entrepreneurs—Who Are They?" p. 5.

29. Grishchenko et al., "A Social Portrait of the Entrepreneur," p. 53; Bunin, "A Social Portrait of the Small and Medium-Sized Business," p. 150; Popov, "Russian Entrepreneurship," p. 96.

30. Bunin, "A Social Portrait of the Small and Medium-Sized Business," p. 150.

31. Perepelkin, "The Russian Entrepreneur," p. 40.

32. Ibid.

33. Ibid.

34. Branko Milanovic, *Poverty, Inequality, and Social Policy in Transiton Economies* (Washington, DC: World Bank, 1995), p. 3.

35. Ol'ga Kryshtanovskaia, "The New Russian Millionaires," *Izvestiia*, September 7, 1994, p. 9.

36. Natal'ia Ershova, "The Transformation of Russia's Ruling Elite Under Conditions of Social Crisis," in Tat'iana Zaslavskaia and L. Arutiunian, eds., *Kuda idet Rossiia? Alternativy obshchestvennogo razvitiia*, vol. 1 (Moscow, 1994), pp. 151–155.

37. Ershova, "The Transformation of Russia's Ruling Elite," p. 154.

38. Ibid.

39. Ibid.

40. Ibid., p. 155. Ershova notes that some two-thirds of "the representatives of Russian business" (presumably including those contained in her sample of the post-Soviet elite) "were not in the circle of those wielding power in the late eighties." On the other hand, some two-thirds of those in the new elite who were currently still associated with the state sector of the economy, "had occupied command posts in the economy earlier" (presumably this refers to their "posts" in the Soviet era).

41. Ol'ga Kryshtanovskaia, "Transformation of the Old Nomenklatura into the New Russian Elite," *Obshchestvennye nauki i sovremennost'*, 1995, no. 1, pp. 60–64.

42. Ol'ga Kryshtanovskaia, "Transformation of the Old Nomenklatura into the New Russian Elite," unpublished report at a conference on "New Russian Elites," Michigan, November 1994.

43. See, for example, Igor' Kukolev, "The Formation of the Business Elite," *Obshchestvennye nauki i sovremennost'*, 1996, no. 2, pp. 12–23.

44. There may be a typographical error in the article by Kryshtanovskaia on which we rely here ("Transformation of the Old Nomenklatura," note 41 above). Table 8 of this article (p. 64) shows that 59 percent of the Yeltsin-era business elite had not earlier been part of the nomenklatura. Tables 10 and 11 of this article (p. 65) show 61 percent of this elite as having been drawn from the nomenklatura, implying that 39 percent had not taken this path.

45. Ibid., pp. 55–57.

46. Ibid., pp. 58–59.

47. *Ekonomicheskie i sotsial'nye peremeny: Monitoring obshchestvennogo mneniia*, 1994, no. 6, pp. 79–80. It is interesting that a larger proportion of worker respondents considered themselves as "losers" rather than "winners" in the privatization process. The opposite was the case among manager respondents. However, the most common response among both groups was "neither winner nor loser."

48. Some illustrations include: Igor Zaslavskii, "The Crisis in Labor and Social Relations," Problems of Economic Transition, vol. 38, (December 1995), no. 8, pp. 50–51; the remarks of Iurii Burtin in the roundtable discussion, "Democracy in Russia: Self-Criticism and Prospects," *Obshchestvennye nauki i sovremennost'*, 1995, no. 2, pp. 42–43; L.A. Beliaeva, ed., *Sotsial'naia stratifikatsiia sovremennogo rossiiskogo obshchestva* (Moscow, 1995), p. 11.

49. Igor Bunin, "Russian Bear's New Clothes," *Financial Times*, September 27, 1994, p. 15.

50. We rely here on Natal'ia Shmatko, "The Formation of the Russian Entrepreneurial System and Bureaucratic Capital," *Sotsiologicheskie issledovaniia*, 1995, no. 6, pp. 32, 34.

51. Freeland et al., "Moscow's Group of Seven."

Notes to Chapter 7

1. Anders Aslund, *How Russia Became a Market Economy* (Washington, DC: Brookings Institution, 1995), p. 17.

2. A review of the VTsIOM survey data can be found in R.V. Ryvkina, "Social Consequences of Economic Reforms," *Sotsiololgicheskii zhurnal*, 1995, no. 3, pp. 27–39.

3. Theda Skocpol, *State and Social Revolution: Analysis of France, Russia and China* (Cambridge: Cambridge University Press, 1979), p. 4.

4. Steven Erlanger, "Moscow Reconstructing Icon of Its Past Glory," *New York Times*, September 26, 1995, pp. 1, 8.

5. These are the words of Anders Aslund, a Swedish economist and adviser to the Gaidar economic reformers. See Anders Aslund, "Almost Anyone Is Better than Yeltsin," *New York Times*, February 13, 1996, p. A18.

6. See the e-mail exchange between the political scientists Jerry Hough and Michael McFaul, August 9, 1996, from Jjohnson@mail.cdu.

7. For a discussion of the "social contract thesis," see Linda Cook, *The Soviet Social Contract and Why It Failed* (Cambridge, MA: Harvard University Press, 1993).

8. Enterprises were taxed when their average wage exceeded a certain level. Layoffs, especially of low-paid workers, tend to raise the average wage of the firm and therefore subject it to a relatively high tax. The excess wage tax was abolished in February 1996.

9. For a discussion of the Russian labor market, see OECD, *Wage-Formation During the Period of Economic Restructuring in the Russian Federation* (Paris: Organization for Economic Cooperation and Development, 1995).

10. For a discussion of trade union development in post-Soviet Russia, see Leonid Gordon, *The Labor Movement in a Transitional Society: A Force For or Against Reform*, unpublished monograph (Hempstead, NY: Center for the Study of Labor and Democracy, Hofstra University, 1995); and Walter D. Connor, "Labor in the New Russia: Four Years On," *Problems of Post-Communism*, vol. 42, (March/April 1995), no. 2, pp. 8–12.

11. Independent union representatives to the Trilateral Commission for Coordination of Social–Labor Relations clashed with the FNDR participants, the former accusing the FNDR representatives of not being true defenders of workers and the FNDR members suggesting that the new unions were apologists of the government. Viktor Chenomyrdin gave the FNDR and some allied unions all the seats on the Trilateral Commission. The Trilateral Commission has not played a significant role in labor–management relations.

12. The average number of hours worked per day fell from 7.2 to 6.9 hours between the first quarter of 1995 and the first quarter of 1996. In industry it fell

from 6.4 to 6.2 hours during this period. *Russian Economic Trends*, vol. 5 (1996), no. 1, p. 100.

13. Ibid., p. 101.

14. *New York Times*, December 11, 1995, p. A6.

15. The poll was conducted by the political scientist Richard Rose in January 1996. For a discussion, see *Time*, May 27, 1996, p. 51.

16. For a discussion of the ideology, see Ralf Dahrendorf, *Reflections on the Revolution in Europe* (London: Chatto and Widus, 1990).

17. V.O. Rukavishnikov, "Sociological Aspects of Modernization in Russia and Other Post-Communist Societies," *Sotsiologicheskie issledovaniia*, 1995, no. 1, p. 42.

18. Robert Skidelsky, *John Maynard Keynes: The Economist as Savior* (New York: Penguin Press, 1992), p. 121.

19. Amartya Sen, *On Ethics and Economics* (Oxford: Basil Blackwell, 1987), pp. 57–58. See also his monographs *Markets and Freedom*, no. 31 (September 1991), and *Beyond Liberalization*, no. 58 (November 1994), International Centre for Economics and Related Disciplines, London School of Economics.

20. Goskomstat, *Uroven zhizni naseleniia Rossii* (Moscow, 1996), p. 173.

21. The U.S. economists are Kenneth Arrow, Lawrence Klein, Wassily Leontief, Robert Solow, and James Tobin. The Russian economists are Leonid Abalkin, Stanislav Shatalin, and Yuri Yaryomenko. Their statement was reported on Radio Free Europe/Radio Liberty, August 12, 1996.

Index

About the Authors

Bertram Silverman is a professor of economics emeritus and director of the Center for the Study of Labor and Democracy at Hofstra University. He has worked as a trade union economist and has organized and directed a joint university–trade union college degree program for working adults. Silverman has written about labor problems in the United States, Latin America, and Europe. He is editor of *Man and Socialism in Cuba: The Great Debate* and co-editor with Murray Yanowitch of *The Worker in "Post-Industrial" Capitalism*; *Labor and Democracy in the Transition to a Market System*; and *Double Shift: Transforming Work in Post-Socialist and Post-Industrial Societies*.

Murray Yanowitch is professor emeritus of economics at Hofstra University. He is the author of numerous works about Soviet social, economic, and labor issues including *Controversies in Soviet Social Thought: Democratization, Social Justice, and the Erosion of Official Ideology*; *Social and Economic Inequality in the Soviet Union: Six Studies*; and *Work in the Soviet Union: Attitudes and Issues*. He is also the editor of *Sociological Research*, a journal of translations of Russian social scientific writings.

DATE DUE

MAR 3 1 1998			
JUL 0 1 1998			
NOV 3 0 1998			
OCT			
NOV 0 0 1998			
NOV 0 8 2003			
MAY 1 3 1999			
MAY 1 9 2000			
			Printed in USA

HIGHSMITH #45230